Connections

Level 4

Columbus, OH

The **McGraw·Hill** Companies

Acknowledgments

Grateful acknowledgment is given to the following publishers and copyright owners for permissions granted to reprint selections from their publications. All possible care has been taken to trace ownership and secure permission for each selection included. In case of any errors or omissions, the Publisher will be pleased to make suitable acknowledgments in future editions.

"The Story of Susan La Flesche Picotte" from Marion Marsh Brown's HOMEWARD THE ARROW'S FLIGHT © 1980. Revised edition 1995. © Field Mouse Productions, Grand Island, Nebraska.

SRAonline.com

Copyright © 2005 SRA/McGraw-Hill.

All rights reserved. Except as permitted under the United States Copyright Act, no part of this publication may be reproduced or distributed in any form or by any means, or stored in a database or retrieval system, without the prior written permission from the publisher, unless otherwise indicated.

Permission is granted to reproduce the material contained on the blackline masters on the condition that such material be reproduced only for classroom use; be provided to students, teachers, or families without charge; and be used solely in conjunction with *Theatre Arts Connections.*

Printed in the United States of America.

Send all inquiries to:
SRA/McGraw-Hill
8787 Orion Place
Columbus, OH 43240-4027

ISBN 0-07-601877-6

4 5 6 7 8 9 QPD 10 09 08 07 06 05

SRA THEATRE ARTS
Connections

Arts Education for the 21st Century

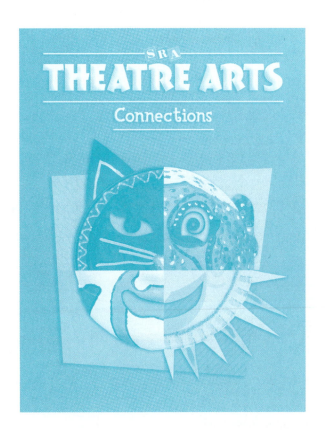

Character   *Culture*   *Plot*   *Critical Thinking*

Creativity   *Literature*   *Personal Expression*

Theatre Arts education encourages different ways of learning, knowing and communicating.

All the Resources you need for a Total Theatre Arts Curriculum

Theatre Arts Connections provides everything teachers need to offer meaningful theatre arts education.

Theatre Arts Connections K–6

Thirty-six 15–30 minute Lessons per grade level develop the elements and principles of theatre arts.

Warm-Up activities focus students on lesson concepts.

Step-by-step teacher instructions promote successful lessons.

Creative Expression quick drama activity in every lesson brings concepts to life.

History and Culture featured in every lesson.

Plus

- **Complete stories and scripts** so teachers have everything they need to be successful
- Unit Openers provide an overview of Unit **concepts and vocabulary** and show theatre's effects across the curriculum.
- Unit Wrap-Up instructions pull unit concepts together as students **create a theatrical production.**
- **Unit Assessments** evaluate understanding.
  - Assessment Rubrics
  - Self-Assessment
  - Quick Quiz
- **Professional Development**

Artsource® Video/DVD

Artsource® Video and DVD offer live performances that apply theatrical elements and principles.

Integrates the four disciplines of art into every lesson

Meet today's standards for theatre arts education.

Perception

Develop concepts about self, human relationships, and the environment using drama elements and theatre conventions.

Creative Expression

Create dramatizations and interpret characters, using voice and body. Apply design, directing, and theatre production concepts and skills.

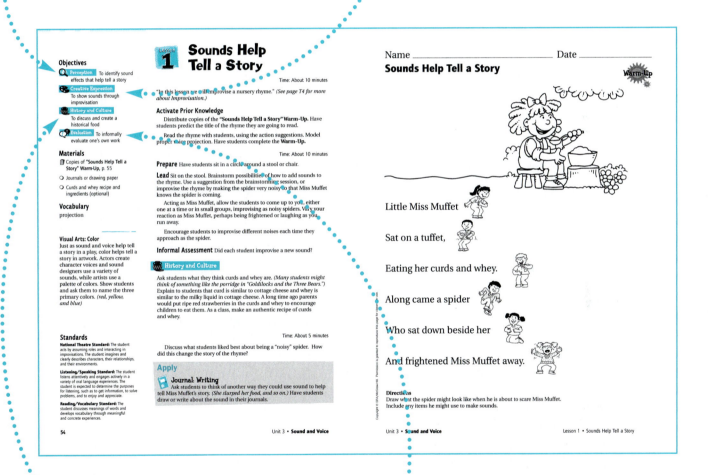

History and Culture

Relate theatre to history, culture, and society.

Evaluation

Respond to and evaluate theatre and theatrical performances.

SRA THEATRE ARTS Connections

Theatre Arts and... Math, Science, Social Studies, Reading and Language Arts

Expand understanding and interest in subject-area studies when students explore theatre arts across the curriculum.

Vocabulary Development Key vocabulary terms are identified and defined to develop the language of theatre.

Reading Themes Make reading themes come to life through dramatic play as students explore a common theme in every unit of *Theatre Arts Connections*.

Theatre's Effects Across the Curriculum Show students how theatre concepts relate to science, math, social studies, reading, and language arts in every unit.

History and Culture Develop historical understanding as students explore theatre history and culture in every lesson.

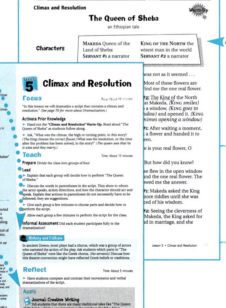

Literature Integration Actively explore literature with stories and scripts from around the world.

Writing Develop writing skills through Journal activities in each lesson.

6

Integrating the Arts

Expose children to music, dance, and visual arts as they explore the theatre arts.

Music

 Artsource® music performances on Video and DVD connect to the elements and principles of theatre.

Visual Arts

Visual Arts connections relate the elements and principles of theatre to the elements and principles of art.

Dance

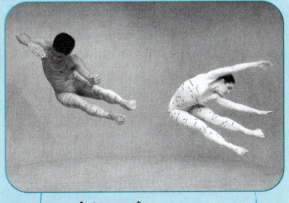

 Artsource® dance performances on Video and DVD help students connect the elements and principles of theatre to professional dance performances.

Case studies have indicated that students perceive "that the arts facilitate their personal and social development." It also appeared that to gain the full benefit of arts education, students should be exposed to all of the arts, including fine arts, dance, theater, and music.

("Arts Education in Secondary School: Effects and Effectiveness" in <u>Critical Links</u>, p. 76)

Connections

Author

Betty Jane Wagner

Betty Jane Wagner is an internationally recognized authority on the educational uses of drama in the classroom and on writing instruction. In 1998, she received the Rewey Belle Inglis Award for Outstanding Woman in English Education from the Women in Literature and Life Assembly of the National Council of Teachers of English. She also received the Judith Kase-Polisini Honorary Research Award for International Drama/Theatre Research from the American Alliance for Theatre and Education.

Recently, she completed a revised edition of *Dorothy Heathcote: Drama as a Learning Medium* (Calendar Islands Publishers, 1999), considered a classic in the field. She wrote *Educational Drama and Language Arts: What Research Shows,* (Heinemann, 1998) and edited *Building Moral Communities Through Educational Drama* (Ablex, 1999).

She co-authored with the late James Moffett three editions of *Student-Centered Language Arts, K–12* (1976, 1983, 1992); and with Mark Larson, *Situations: A Case Book of Virtual Realities for the English Teacher* (1995). She has written several curricula, including *Interaction, Language Roundup,* and *Books at Play,* a drama and literacy program. She has also written numerous chapters in books, such as the *Handbook of Research on Teaching the English Language Arts* and *Perspectives on Talk and Learning,* as well as articles for the National Council of Teachers of English journals.

Wagner is a professor in the Language and Literacy Program of the College of Education at Roosevelt University and director of the Chicago Area Writing Project.

The McGraw-Hill Companies

McGraw-Hill: Your Fine-Arts Partner for K–12 Art and Music

McGraw-Hill offers textbook programs to build, support, and extend an enriching fine-arts curriculum from Kindergarten through high school.

**Senior Author
Rosalind Ragans**

Start with Art SRA

SRA/McGraw-Hill presents *Art Connections* for Grades K–6. *Art Connections* builds the foundations of the elements and principles of art across the grade levels as the program integrates art history and culture, aesthetic perception, creative expression in art production, and art criticism into every lesson.

Art Connections also develops strong cross-curricular connections and integrates the arts with literature, *Theatre Arts Connections* lessons, *Artsource®* experiences, and integrated music selections from Macmillan/McGraw-Hill's *Spotlight on Music.*

**Author
Rosalind Ragans
and Gene Mittler**

Integrate with Art Glencoe

Glencoe/McGraw-Hill offers comprehensive middle and high school art programs that encourage students to make art a part of their lifelong learning. All Glencoe art programs interweave the elements and principles of art to help students build perceptual skills, promote creative expression, explore historical and cultural heritage, and evaluate artwork.

**Author
Rosalind Ragans**

- Introduce students to the many themes artists express.
- Explore the media, techniques, and processes of art.
- Understand the historical and cultural contexts of art.

ArtTalk offers high school students opportunities to perceive, create, appreciate, and evaluate art as it develops the elements and principles of art.

Motivate with Music Macmillan McGraw-Hill

Macmillan/McGraw-Hill's *Spotlight on Music* offers an exiting and comprehensive exposure to music foundations and appreciation.

Sing with Style Glencoe

Glencoe/McGraw-Hill introduces *Experiencing Choral Music* for Grades 6–12. This multilevel choral music program includes instruction in the basic skills of vocal production and music literacy, and provides expertly recorded music selections in many different styles and from various periods in history.

THEATRE ARTS
Connections

At every grade level units develop...
- Plot
- Character
- Sound and Voice
- Visual Elements
- Movement
- Subject, Theme, and Mood

Activities
- Theatre Games
- Improvisation
- Pantomime
- Tableau
- Puppetry
- Playwriting
- Reader's Theatre
- Costumes
- Props
- Masks
- Direction

Helps students...
- Understand the **elements** of drama and the **conventions** of theatre.
- Explore **history and culture** through dramatic play.
- Experience literary elements of **plot, setting, and character**.
- Apply design, directing, and **theatre production** skills.
- Develop **critical thinking** and analysis.

Standards
- Meets National and State Standards for Theatre Arts
- Reinforces key subject-area standards in Reading and Language Arts, Listening and Speaking, Social Studies, Science, and Mathematics

Getting Started
The very basics...

Here are some tips for Getting Started with Theatre Arts Connections.

Before School Begins

1. Explore the program components.
2. Plan your year.
   - Consider how often you meet with students. ***Theatre Arts Connections*** is designed to be a rewarding 15–30 minute weekly activity.
   - Decide how many lessons you can present.
   - Examine your curriculum requirements.
   - Select the lessons that best meet your curriculum requirements.

The First Day of School

1. Give an overview of your goals for theatre arts education.
2. Establish and communicate rules for behavior.

Planning a Lesson

1. Review the lesson in the **Teacher's Edition,** including lesson objectives, in-text questions, and *Creative Expression* activities.
2. Make copies of activities or assessments that will be needed for the lesson.
3. Determine how you will assess the lesson.

> "I am enough of an artist to draw freely upon my imagination. Imagination is more important than knowledge. Knowledge is limited. Imagination encircles the world."
>
> —Albert Einstein (1879-1955), physicist

Table of Contents

Program Overview 3

UNIT 1 Plot

Visual Arts: Line • Reading Theme: Risks and Consequences

Unit Opener 16

Lesson	Creative Expression	Story	
❶ Plot and Sequence	Play a theatre game		18
➥ ❷ Plot and the Five *W*s	Use improvisation		20
❸ A Plot Presents a Problem	Tell a story	"A Sly Cat"	22
➥ ❹ Conflict and Complications	Dramatize a story	"Li and the Dragon"	24
❺ Climax and Resolution	Create a tableau	"Remember the Alamo"	26
➥ ❻ Unit Activity: Dramatized Literary Selection	Dramatize a story	"Adventure in the Wild Wood" from *The Wind in the Willows*	28

UNIT 2 Character

Visual Arts: Shape, Pattern, Rhythm, and Movement • Reading Theme: Dollars and Sense

Unit Opener 34

Lesson	Creative Expression	Story	
❶ Characters Act and Feel	Use dramatic movement	"The Milkmaid and her Pail" from *Aesop's Fables*	36
❷ Characters Relate	Create a tableau	"The Bag of Gold"	38
❸ Characters Want Something	Use improvisation		40
➥ ❹ Action and Inaction	Use improvisation	"The Battle of Picacho Pass"	42
➥ ❺ Characters Solve a Problem	Dramatize a story	"The Golden Goose" from *Grimm's Fairy Tales*	44
➥ ❻ Unit Activity: Scripted Monologue	Write and perform a monologue	"The Barber's Clever Wife"	46

➥ Indicates Core Lesson

UNIT 3 Movement

Visual Arts: Color and Value • Reading Theme: From Mystery to Medicine

Unit Opener 52

Lesson	Creative Expression	Story	
❶ Movement Snapshots	Create a tableau		54
❷ Movement and the Five *W*s	Use dramatic movement	"Bending Willow"	56
❸ Shapes in Movement	Use creative movement	"The Microbe"	58
❹ Rhythm and Repetition	Use dramatic movement		60
❺ Action and Reaction	Use pantomime		62
❻ Unit Activity: Dramatized Literary Selection	Perform a pantomime	"The Story of Susan La Flesche Picotte" from *Homeward the Arrow's Flight*	64

UNIT 4 Sound and Voice

Visual Arts: Form, Texture, and Emphasis • Reading Theme: Survival

Unit Opener 70

Lesson	Creative Expression	Story	
❶ Sound and the Five *W*s	Create sound effects		72
❷ Sound Shows Setting	Play a theatre game	"Jabberwocky" from *Through the Looking Glass*	74
❸ Character Voices	Tell a story	"Storytellers at Sea" from *Captains Courageous*	76
❹ Sound Creates Feelings	Create sound effects	"Keep Your Eye on the Sun" from "Music and Slavery"	78
❺ Tone and Inflection	Use improvisation	"Planning for the North Pole"	80
❻ Unit Activity: Dramatized Literary Selection	Use sound effects and voice in a dramatization	"On Mars!" from *A Princess of Mars*	82

UNIT 5 Visual Elements

Visual Arts: Space, Proportion, and Distortion • **Reading Theme:** Communication

Unit Opener 88

Lesson	Creative Expression	Story	
➊ Setting	Create a setting		90
➋ Props	Create props	"The Telephone is Born"	92
➌ Visual Elements and the Five *W*s	Create a setting	"The Burning of the Rice Fields"	94
➍ Costumes	Create costumes		96
➎ Masks and Makeup	Create a mask		98
➏ Unit Activity: Improvisation	Use visual elements	"Animal Language" from *The Story of Dr. Doolittle*	100

UNIT 6 Subject, Theme, and Mood

Visual Arts: Balance, Harmony, Variety, and Unity • **Reading Theme:** A Changing America

Unit Opener 106

Lesson	Creative Expression	Story	
➊ Subject, Theme, and the Five *W*s	Create a tableau		108
➋ Finding Theme	Use dramatic movement	"I Hear America Singing"	110
➌ Showing Mood	Design costumes		112
➍ A Director Shows Theme	Use improvisation	"The Mystery of Roanoke Island"	114
➎ Actors Can Show Mood	Create a tableau		116
➏ Unit Activity: Scripted Play	Write and perform a script		118

➥ Indicates Core Lesson

Activity Stories **124**

Answer Key and Spanish Vocabulary List **139**

Teacher's Handbook

Table of Contents T1

Introduction T2

Theatre Technique Tips T3

Professional Development Articles T21

Scope and Sequence of Theatre Concepts T31

Scope and Sequence of Theatre Activities T34

Program Glossary T35

Program Index T38

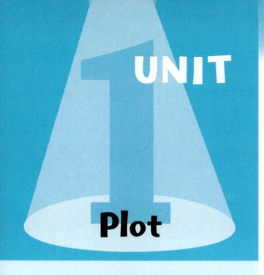

UNIT 1
Plot

Unit Overview

Lesson 1 • Plot and Sequence
The events in a plot occur in a specific sequence. *Theatre Game*

Lesson 2 • Plot and the Five Ws
The details of a plot usually answer the five Ws—who, what, where, when, and why. *Improvisation*

Lesson 3 • A Plot Presents a Problem Characters in a drama or story wrestle with a central problem. *Storytelling*

Lesson 4 • Conflict and Complications Conflict in a plot grows. Complications, or new twists, make the central problem harder to solve. *Dramatization*

Lesson 5 • Climax and Resolution The climax, or high point, of a plot marks the turning point in the action; usually problems are resolved during the resolution. *Tableau*

Lesson 6 • Unit Activity: Dramatized Literary Selection This activity will give students the opportunity to show elements of plot in a dramatized literary selection.

See pages T3–T20 for more about **Theatre Technique Tips.**

Introduce Unit Concepts

"A plot is the order of events in a story or drama. The people or animals in a plot come up against a problem. The plot has a climax, or high point, after which the problems are usually solved." **"Una trama es el orden de eventos en una historia o drama. Los personajes, personas o animales, se encuentran con un problema. La trama tiene un clímax, o punto culminate, después de que normalmente se resuelven los problemas."**

Plot

▶ Ask students to brainstorm different types of problems people or animals in a story or play might have. *(They can fight; a person can lose something important or be fooled; and so on.)*

▶ Have students describe the order of events of a favorite story, book, or movie. Do the people in the story have problems? How do they solve them?

Vocabulary

plot trama—an ordered group of events in a story, book, or drama

climax clímax—the turning point or high point of a plot

resolution resolución—the part of a plot, usually near the end, in which the plot's problems are worked out

Unit Links

Visual Arts: Line
▶ Remind students that artists can use many kinds of lines. Explain that feelings created in different parts of a plot can be illustrated through lines. Ask students what kinds of lines might show the part of a plot when problems are solved. *(smooth lines)*

▶ Show students the image of an artwork containing lines, such as *Maquillage* by Natalia Goncharova. What lines do they see? *(straight, diagonal)* Are these lines full of movement or are they calm and peaceful? *(movement)* Have students compare and contrast the way calm and peaceful feelings and ideas are depicted in art and theatre.

Reading Theme: Risks and Consequences
▶ Ask students to think of a time when they took a risk in order to help someone, such as standing up for a friend who was being teased. What happened? *(I got teased too, and so on.)*

▶ Name a book or story with which students are familiar, such as *Mrs. Frisby and the Rats of NIMH*, and choose a character who took a risk, such as Mrs. Frisby. What was one risk that character took? *(She went to see the owl.)* Have students describe the positive and negative consequences.

Teacher Background

Background on Plot

Plot is the sequence of events in a story or drama. The action in a plot can be defined as everything the characters do. Thus plot is the selection, arrangement, and progression of action from the beginning to the end of a story or drama. Most interesting stories or dramas have a central problem, complications, a climax, and a resolution.

Background on Playwriting

Playwriting involves developing a new plot or adapting an existing plot in a way that will be portrayed by actors. A playwright creates characters whose words and actions move the plot forward; he or she also writes dialogue for actors and sometimes indicates how an actor should move or speak. All parts of a script should help communicate the plot to the audience and move it forward.

Research in Theatre Education

". . . dramatic play is a vehicle whereby children can both practice and learn about literacy skills and begin to develop 'storying' skills which might be used in story writing."

—Jennifer Ross Goodman

"A Naturalistic Study of the Relationship Between Literacy Development and Dramatic Play in Five-Year-Old Children"

Differentiated Instruction

Reteach

Have students choose their favorite movie and describe its plot using the five *W*s.

Challenge

Have students choose a section from the plot of a book they recently read. Have them dramatize it for other students, and ask the other students to identify whether this part of the plot shows the central problem's introduction, new complications, the climax, or the resolution.

Special Needs

Encourage active participation of students with disabilities by allowing them to propose ideas for the content of class or group dramatizations.

Theatre's Effects Across the Curriculum

★ **Reading/Writing**
Writing Comprehension Expressing ideas in their journals gives students practice in recording, developing, and reflecting their ideas.

★ **Math**
Ordering When students compare and portray actions in a sequence, they are exercising comparison and ordering skills similar to those used with numbers in mathematics.

★ **Science**
Cause and Effect As students study the sequence of events in a plot, they review the ways chains of events occur in plots and in the natural world.

★ **Social Studies**
History Dramatizing historical events gives students a chance to look at these events through different points of view.

★ **Music**
Point of View Students better understand an historical event when they explore different points of view by singing or listening to songs written from different perspectives or by exploring the voices of different characters.

★ **Dance**
Teamwork When students work in groups in dramatic activities, they use similar skills utilized when dancing with a partner or in a group.

Unit 1 • Plot

Objectives

Perception To identify events that form a sequence

Creative Expression To show the sequence of steps in a common task by playing a theatre game

History and Culture To think about cultural celebrations of events in the sequence of growing up

Evaluation To informally evaluate one's own work

Materials
- Copies of **"Plot and Sequence" Warm-Up,** p. 19
- Journals or writing paper

Vocabulary
plot
sequence

Standards

National Theatre Standard: The student acts by assuming roles and interacting in improvisations. The student is expected to assume roles that exhibit concentration and contribute to the action of classroom dramatizations based on personal experience and heritage, imagination, literature, and history.

Listening/Speaking Standard: The student responds to speakers by asking questions, making contributions, and paraphrasing what is said.

Writing Standard: The student writes for a variety of audiences and purposes, and in a variety of forms. The student is expected to write to express, discover, record, develop, reflect in ideas, and to problem solve.

Lesson 1: Plot and Sequence

Focus
Time: About 10 minutes

"In this lesson we will play a theatre game to show a sequence of events." *(See page T5 for more about Theatre Games.)*

Activate Prior Knowledge

▶ Hand out the **"Plot and Sequence" Warm-Up,** and have students complete it.

▶ Discuss student answers. Say, "This story shows a chain of events. What event caused the problem Carmen faced?" *(She stayed up too late working on her report.)*

Teach
Time: About 15 minutes

Prepare Divide students into small groups.

Lead Tell students that each group will act out steps of an everyday task; each member will perform one step at a time. As an example, show the steps needed to shoot a basketball, demonstrating steps students may forget, such as picking up the basketball.

▶ Assign one of the following to each group: making a bed, making lunch, getting ready for bed. Have each group identify and apply personal observations of its tasks and divide up the steps.

▶ Have each group perform its task. Ask the class to guess the task.

Informal Assessment Did each student act out a step in the correct sequence?

History and Culture

Explain that the process of growing up is an example of sequence of events. Say, "Most cultures celebrate the sequence of growing up. For example, many Puerto Ricans and Mexicans hold a special party, called a *quinceañera*, to mark a girl's fifteenth birthday." Explain that this party celebrates the girl's moving from childhood into adulthood.

Reflect
Time: About 5 minutes

▶ Ask students what made some tasks easier to identify than others.

Apply

Journal: Sequencing
In their journals, have each student write an outline for a story about a risk he or she once took, focusing on the sequence of events.

Name _____ Date _____

Plot and Sequence

Warm-Up

Some events have been left out of the story below. Read the story and think about what events might have led to the next event. Write your ideas for these events in the blanks below.

Carmen rolled over in bed. Why hadn't her alarm gone off yet? Something felt wrong. She looked up at her clock and saw—

"7:45!" Carmen yelled. *"¡Estoy tarde!* I'm going to be late!"

Leaping out of bed, Carmen quickly got dressed. She should not have stayed up so late last night working on her report. What else did she need to do to get ready?

She _____
_____
_____
_____
_____
_____.

Where was her report? It was due today! She looked _____
_____
_____
_____
_____
_____.

There it was! She grabbed her report, called good-bye to her mother, and ran out the door to school. If she ran fast enough, she might not be late after all.

Objectives

 Perception To identify ways the five *W*s can reveal plot

 Creative Expression To communicate *who* and *what* using improvised knocking

 History and Culture To learn one way improvisational actors use the five *W*s

 Evaluation To informally evaluate one's own work

Materials

- Copies of **"Plot and the Five *W*s" Warm-Up,** p. 21
- Journals or writing paper

Vocabulary

improvisation

Standards

National Theatre Standard: The student acts by assuming roles and interacting in improvisations. The student is expected to assume roles that exhibit concentration and contribute to the action of classroom dramatizations based on personal experience and heritage, imagination, literature, and history.

Listening/Speaking Standard: The student interprets speakers' messages (both verbal and nonverbal), purposes, and perspectives.

Writing Standard: The student writes for a variety of audiences and purposes, and in a variety of forms. The student is expected to write to inform such as to explain, describe, report, and narrate.

Lesson 2: Plot and the Five Ws

Focus
Time: About 10 minutes

"In this lesson we will use improvisation to show *who* and *what*." (See page T4 for more about Improvisation.)

Activate Prior Knowledge

▶ Hand out the **"Plot and the Five *W*s" Warm-Up,** and have students complete it.

▶ Say, "This picture shows people escaping slavery using the Underground Railroad, which was a system of houses in which people hid on their way to freedom." What clues in the picture helped students guess the five *W*s? *(clothing, looks on people's faces, and so on)* Explain that most plots answer the five *W*s.

Teach
Time: About 15 minutes

Prepare Students should remain seated.

Lead Tell students that one student at a time will decide on a *who* and *what*. He or she will stay out of sight of the class and knock on a table as if knocking on a door. The goal is to communicate the *who* and *what* through the knocking. Possible *who*s and *what*s include a child going to visit a friend, a person with an important message, and so on.

▶ Have volunteers perform this improvisation. Have the rest of the class guess, and then have volunteers repeat their knocking and add speech.

Informal Assessment Did each student improvise and/or guess the *who* and *what*?

 History and Culture

Tell students that Viola Spolin founded America's first improvisational acting company in 1946. Sometimes improvisational actors establish a few of the five *W*s ahead of time but will then make up answers to the others as they improvise. Have students compare Viola Spolin and her contributions with those of an improvisational actor such as Mike Meyers.

Reflect
Time: About 5 minutes

▶ Ask, "Was it challenging to use knocking to show *who* and *what*? Why?" *(yes, because I couldn't explain anything, and so on)*

Apply

 Journal: Describing
In their journals, have students use the five *W*s to describe a favorite thing they do on the weekend.

Name _____ Date _____

Plot and the Five Ws

Look at the picture below. Use the picture to answer the following questions.

1. Who are these people?

_____

2. What are they doing?

_____

3. When might this be taking place?

_____

4. Where might this be taking place?

_____

5. Why do you think they are doing these things?

_____

Objectives

🔍 **Perception** To identify problems presented in a plot

🎨 **Creative Expression** To create a central problem using dramatic storytelling

🏺 **History and Culture** To identify some functions and examples of oral literature

💬 **Evaluation** To informally evaluate one's own work

Materials

- Copies of **"A Plot Presents a Problem" Warm-Up,** p. 23
- Journals or writing paper

Unit Links

Visual Arts: Line
Lines can illustrate different kinds of problems. Discuss with students the kinds of lines that could illustrate types of problems; for example, a confusing group of problems could be illustrated with a tangled mess of lines while one big problem could be shown with a line that goes straight up and then swoops down.

Standards

National Theatre Standard: The student is expected to identify and compare similar characters and situations in stories and dramas from and about various cultures, illustrate with classroom dramatizations, and discuss how theatre reflects life.

Listening/Speaking Standard: The student listens and speaks both to gain and share knowledge of his/her own culture, the culture of others, and the common elements of cultures. The student is expected to compare oral traditions across regions and cultures.

Math Standard: The student uses logical reasoning to make sense of his or her world.

22

Lesson 3: A Plot Presents a Problem

Focus
Time: About 10 minutes

"In this lesson we will use storytelling to tell a story with a central problem." *(See page T11 for more about Storytelling.)*

Activate Prior Knowledge
▶ Hand out the **"A Plot Presents a Problem" Warm-Up,** and have students complete it. Discuss student's answers.

Teach
Time: About 15 minutes

Prepare Divide students into small groups.

Lead Tell students that each group will use storytelling to tell "A Sly Cat." One group member will be the storyteller; the others will be cat(s) or mice. The storyteller should not speak dialogue but should pause to allow actors to act it out.

▶ Ask the groups to change the story's problem; for example, what if the cat became friends with the mice and stopped chasing them?

▶ Give the groups time to plan, and then have them perform for the class.

Informal Assessment Did each group work together to tell the story, demonstrate a logical connection of events, and change its central problem?

 History and Culture

Explain that most cultures tell stories that teach lessons or explain customs. The Ga people, from whom "A Sly Cat" comes, tell the following story about their Homowo Festival: the Ga traveled for many years and suffered with little food before reaching Africa's west coast. When they overcame that problem, they celebrated this festival. Have students compare central problems in stories from their own families with the central problem in this story.

Reflect
Time: About 5 minutes

▶ Have each group describe its characters, their relationships, and the environment in which their story took place. Have them compare and contrast each group's new central problem with the Ga's cultural version. Which did they like best?

Apply

📓 **Journal: Personal Writing**
In their journals, have students describe a time they encountered a problem, such as losing something, and how they solved it.

Unit 1 • Plot

Name _____ Date _____

A Plot Presents a Problem

Read the paragraphs, and then answer the questions below.

A Sly Cat
a Ghanian fable

Once there was a sly and tricky cat. When she was young and strong, she caught many mice, and all the mice were terrified of her. But when she grew older, she could not catch mice anymore.

One day the sly cat thought, "Since I cannot use my speed to catch these mice, I will use a trick instead." So the cat lay on her back and did not move at all. A mouse saw her. "The cat is dead!" the mouse thought.

The mouse ran to her friends and said, "The cat is dead! Let us dance and play!"

Full of joy, the mice began to dance and play. They danced round, and round the cat, but the cat did not move. Then one of the mice jumped on the cat's head.

"Look at me!" he said. "The bad cat is dead! Let us dance on her head!"

Quick as a flash the cat jumped up and caught the silly mouse! The other mice ran away squeaking with fear.

Moral: Mice, never believe a cat!

1. What is the main problem in the plot?

_____

_____

2. Who takes a risk?

_____

_____

_____

3. What is the consequence of the risk?

_____

_____

_____

Unit 1 • **Plot**   Lesson 3 • A Plot Presents a Problem

Objectives

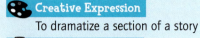
Perception To identify conflict and complications in stories

Creative Expression To dramatize a section of a story

History and Culture To identify themes of Chinese folktales and drama

Evaluation To informally evaluate one's own work

Materials
○ Journals or writing paper

Vocabulary
conflict
complications

Standards

National Theatre Standard: The student acts by assuming roles and interacting in improvisations. The student is expected to assume roles that exhibit concentration and contribute to the action of classroom dramatizations based on personal experience and heritage, imagination, literature, and history.

Listening/Speaking Standard: The student understands that language formality varies according to situations and audiences. The student varies language according to situation, audience, and purpose (for example, appropriate tone, content, vocabulary).

Reading Standard: The student expresses and supports responses to various types of text. The student is expected to offer observations, make connections, react, speculate, interpret, and raise questions in response to texts.

Lesson 4: Conflict and Complications

Focus
Time: About 10 minutes

"In this lesson we will dramatize sections of a folktale in which conflict or complications are introduced." *(See page T6 for more about Dramatization.)*

Activate Prior Knowledge

▶ Explain that struggles between characters are called conflict; complications are twists that make the central problem harder to solve.

▶ Read aloud **"Li and the Dragon."** Discuss who Li is in conflict with and the plot's complications. *(his brother and mother; Li's brother steals things; his mother doesn't believe him)*

Teach
Time: About 15 minutes

Prepare Divide students into three groups. Have students create a playing space.

Lead Tell students that each group will dramatize a section of "Li and the Dragon." Students who are not playing a central character should create new characters or act as objects in the setting, such as trees. As traditional Chinese drama focused on beautiful, interesting language, challenge them to use poetic, formal speech. Model this, saying, "Oh, great dragon, I thank you for this wondrous stick."

▶ Assign one of the following to each group: the beginning and horse section, the rooster section, and the stick section. Allow five minutes for planning.

▶ In sequence, have each group perform.

Informal Assessment Did each group work together to show conflict and complications in a section of the story?

History and Culture

Tell students that many Chinese folktales are thousands of years old. The folktales' plots teach Chinese values such as the triumph of justice over injustice or of wisdom over physical strength. Some of these same themes appeared in traditional Chinese drama as well.

Reflect
Time: About 5 minutes

▶ Have students compare and contrast their interpretations and describe the characters and their relationships.

Apply

Journal: Describing
Explain that the phrase "a willing suspension of disbelief" refers to an audience's willingness to pretend that a play or movie's events are real. Have students describe conflicts or complications from a favorite movie in their journals, comparing and contrasting them with events in real life and explaining whether students could suspend disbelief.

Unit 1 • Plot

Li and the Dragon

a Chinese folktale

Long ago in China there lived a kind boy named Li. Li gave his food to the poor, but his mother did not like this. "Go work for your brother Chu," she said.

On the road to Chu's house Li saw a snake laying half dead in the grass. He felt sorry for it, so he fed it his rice cakes.

"Thank you," hissed the snake. "Will you put me in the river?"

"Of course," Li said, and he did. Light flashed, and the snake became a river dragon!

"Do not be afraid," the dragon said. "You will find a horse in the bushes over there. Tell it, 'Neigh, neigh,' and you will see its value."

Li found the horse. "Neigh, neigh," he said, and out of the horse's mouth fell three gold coins!

Li thanked the dragon and he went to his brother Chu's house to stay the night. He left the horse in Chu's shed, saying, "Whatever you do, don't say, 'Neigh, neigh' to the horse."

Chu snuck out that night and said, "Neigh, neigh," to the horse. Three gold coins dropped out of its mouth! In the morning Chu gave his brother another horse. When Li took it home and said, "Neigh, neigh," to it, nothing happened.

"You foolish boy," his mother said. "There are no coins. Go work for your brother."

Li saw the river dragon on his way to Chu's house. "Take the rooster in those bushes," said the dragon. "Tell it, 'Cock-a-doodle-doo,' and you will see its value."

Li took the rooster from the bushes. "Cock-a-doodle-doo," he said, and out of the rooster's mouth fell three silver coins!

After thanking the dragon, Li went to his brother Chu's house. He put the rooster in Chu's shed, saying, "Whatever you do, don't say, 'Cock-a-doodle-doo,' to it."

Well of course Chu snuck out that night and said, "Cock-a-doodle-doo," to the rooster. When he saw the silver coins, he hid the rooster. The next day he gave Li one of his own roosters. When Li took the rooster home and said, "Cock-a-doodle-doo," to it, nothing happened.

Once more Li went down the road to Chu's house, and on his way he saw the river dragon. "Take the stick by that bush," said the dragon. "Say to it, 'Dance, stick, dance.' When you want it to stop, say 'Teng.'"

Li took the stick and said, "Dance, stick, dance." The stick began beating his legs. "Teng!" he cried, and the stick lay still.

After thanking the dragon, Li went again to his brother's house. "I will leave this stick in your shed," Li said to Chu, "but be sure you do not say to it, 'Dance, stick, dance.'"

Chu snuck out to the shed. "Dance, stick, dance," he said. The stick began beating him around the legs! "Help, help," he cried, and Li, who had been hiding, went to his brother.

Li agreed to help him in exchange for his horse and rooster. After Li stopped the stick, Chu gave back the dragon's gifts, and Li and his mother lived comfortably for the rest of their days.

Objectives

 Perception To identify examples of climax and resolution

 Creative Expression To create a tableau showing the climax of the battle of the Alamo

 History and Culture To identify and compare the climax of favorite movies

 Evaluation To informally evaluate one's own work

Materials
- Copies of **"Climax and Resolution" Warm-Up,** p. 27
- Journals or writing paper

Vocabulary
climax
resolution

Unit Links

Visual Arts: Line
Lines can illustrate climax and resolution. Have each student illustrate the concepts using a line. Remind them that the climax is the highest point of excitement in a story, and the resolution is when problems are put to rest. Have students explain their line choices.

Standards

National Theatre Standard: The student collaborates to select interrelated characters, environments, and situations for classroom dramatizations.

Listening/Speaking Standard: The student listens and speaks both to gain and share knowledge of his/her own culture, the culture of others, and the common elements of cultures.

Social Studies/History Standard: The student is expected to analyze the causes, major events, and effects of the Texas Revolution, including the battles of the Alamo and San Jacinto.

Lesson 5: Climax and Resolution

Focus
Time: About 10 minutes

"In this lesson we will use our bodies to create monuments that illustrate a battle's climax." *(See page T7 for more about Tableau.)*

Activate Prior Knowledge

▶ Hand out the **"Climax and Resolution" Warm-Up.** Tell students to read the quote and answer the questions as best they can.

▶ Explain to students that this battle took place in 1836 during Texas's war for independence from Mexico. Tell them that although Mexico won this battle, this battle was the turning point in the war. It inspired Texans to fight even harder, and they won the war.

▶ Tell students that the climax of a story is its turning point, and that the resolution, or working out of problems, takes place after the climax. Ask students if this battle was the climax or resolution of Texas's war for independence. *(climax)*

Teach
Time: About 15 minutes

Prepare Divide students into groups.

Lead Say, "Each group is a planning committee given the task of creating a monument or statue to be placed in front of the Alamo. This monument should show the climax of the battle for the Alamo."

▶ Tell the groups that they will create their monuments using their bodies. Give the groups five minutes to plan their monuments.

▶ Have the class be silent. As you ask each group to show its monument, say, "And in front of the Alamo there was a monument."

Informal Assessment Did each group's monument highlight the battle's possible climax?

 History and Culture

Explain to students that another way to define *climax* is to think of it as the most exciting part of a story. Ask students to compare the battle for the Alamo to climaxes of favorite movies, such as *Holes*. How do such events in real life differ from those in fiction?

Reflect
Time: About 5 minutes

▶ Ask each group what emotion they were trying to express through their monument. How did each monument make others feel?

Apply

 Journal: Personal Writing
Have students write a story about a struggle in their own lives, including a climax and resolution, in their journals.

Name _____ Date _____

Climax and Resolution

Read the paragraph and then answer the questions below.

Remember the Alamo

"Under the cover of darkness [the Mexican army] approached . . . and planting their scaling ladders against our walls just as light was approaching, they climbed up to the tops of our walls and jumped down within . . . As fast as the front ranks were slain, they were filled up again by fresh troops. The Mexicans numbered several thousands while there were only one hundred and eighty-two Texans."

—Susan Hanning Dickenson,
in *History of Texas*
by James M. Morphis

1. Who fought in the battle of the Alamo?

_____
_____
_____
_____

2. Who do you think won the battle of the Alamo?

_____
_____
_____
_____

3. Why might people make a monument to remember this battle?

_____
_____
_____
_____

Objectives

 Perception To review the elements of plot and to connect the concept of conflict to real life

Creative Expression To dramatize the plot of a literary selection

 History and Culture To compare the risk Mole took in "Adventure in the Wild Wood" with other stories of risk they have read

 Evaluation To thoughtfully and honestly evaluate own participation using the four steps of criticism

Materials

- Copies of **"Adventure in the Wild Wood,"** pp. 124–126
- Copies of the **Unit 1 Self-Criticism Questions,** p. 32
- Copies of the **Unit 1 Quick Quiz,** p. 33
- *Artsource*® Performing Arts Resource Package (optional)

Standards

National Theatre Standard: The student identifies and compares similar characters and situations in stories and dramas from and about various cultures, illustrates with classroom dramatizations, and discusses how theatre reflects life.

28

 Lesson 6

Unit Activity: Dramatized Literary Selection

Focus
Time: About 10 minutes

Review Unit Concepts

"Plot is the main story in a play, book, or story. A plot's events happen in a particular sequence. The central problem and conflict in a plot are made worse through complications. The climax is the turning point in a plot; during the resolution, problems are usually solved." **"La trama es la historia principal de una obra dramática, libro o cuento. Los eventos de la trama ocurren en una secuencia particular. El problema central y conflicto en la trama se dificultan a través de unas complicaciones. El clímax es el punto culminante de la trama; durante la resolucíon normalmente se resuelven los problemas."**

▶ Review with students the different elements of plot they dramatized in this unit.

▶ Review the unit vocabulary on page 16.

 History and Culture

"Adventure in the Wild Wood" is a selection from the fictional adventure story *The Wind in the Willows*. Have students think of another book they have read in which a character takes a risk. Does either character act in a way the student would act? Ask them to write a paragraph describing the plot, including the risk a character took and the consequences of the risk. Have them end by comparing their participation in the dramatization of "Adventure in the Wild Wood" to the story they chose.

Classroom Management Tips

The following are tips for managing your classroom during the **Rehearsals** and **Activity:**

✔ **Set Ground Rules** Tell students to respect each others' ideas and contributions. Explain that if they cannot participate appropriately, they will have to sit at their desks. Seeing the other students having fun may help them choose to follow the ground rules next time.

✔ **Encourage Creativity** Tell students to stick to the main idea of the plot, but not to be afraid to be creative and original in their interpretations.

Unit 1 • **Plot**

Teach

Time: One 25-minute rehearsal period
One 10-minute rehearsal period
One 15-minute activity period

First Rehearsal

▶ Distribute **"Adventure in the Wild Wood"** on pages 124–126, and read the story aloud while students follow along. Discuss the story's five *W*s, central problem, complications, climax, and resolution.

▶ Reread aloud the summary at the excerpt's beginning. Say, "Rat has seen a lot more of the world than Mole. What risk does Mole take?" *(He goes out alone into the Wild Wood.)* Discuss possible consequences.

▶ Divide students into pairs. Tell each pair to improvise the conversation in which Rat tells Mole about Badger and the dangerous Wild Wood. How does each animal speak and move? Does Mole decide immediately to go anyway?

▶ As time allows, have each pair share its improvisation for the class. Discuss the characters' relationships and differences between the improvisations.

Second Rehearsal

▶ Divide students into groups of six. Have each group choose one member to play Mole; have other group members form a circle around Mole.

▶ Have students describe the environment of the Wild Wood. Reread the story's description of the faces, whistling, and pattering. Say, "The students in each circle will create the sights and sounds of the Wild Wood. When I say, 'Then the faces began,' you will silently make faces. When I say, 'Then the whistling began,' you will make scary whistling noises. When I say, 'Then the pattering began,' you will use your bodies to make pattering noises. Each student playing Mole should react."

▶ Say the three sentences above, leaving time for dramatization. If time allows, repeat and allow other students to play Mole.

Plot Activity

▶ Have students create room for the **Activity**. Divide students into groups of three. Have each group assign the roles of Mole, Rat, and Badger.

▶ Say, "The story ends before Mole and Rat go home. What if, before they get home, Mole and Rat somehow come into contact with Badger? Is Badger happy to see them? What happens next?" Tell each group to dramatize the story, beginning with Rat's realization of Mole's absence. *(See page T6 for more about Dramatization.)* Explain that when they get to the end of the story, they should imagine and dramatize the way Mole and Rat meet up with Badger.

▶ Give groups time to dramatize this sequence, saying "freeze," when you want them to stop.

▶ Have students develop criteria for the **Activity**. Have students apply these criteria to their own performances.

Standards

National Theatre Standard: The student acts by assuming roles and interacting in improvisations. The student is expected to imagine and clearly describe characters, their relationships, and their environments.

Unit Links

Visual Arts: Line
Lines can illustrate feelings created by different parts of a plot. Ask students what feelings are created by the complications in "Adventure in the Wild Wood." *(fear, terror)* Have students create simple line drawings of Mole's fearful face. Discuss the kinds of lines students used to show fear. Have students compare them with the movements they used and they saw others use in the **Plot Activity**.

Theatrical Arts Connection

Television Describe an episode from a television show with which students are familiar. Ask students to describe the plot of the episode using the five *W*s. Discuss why the writers might have chosen these five *W*s. Did any of them make the show funnier or more interesting to audiences? How do they reflect modern American culture?

Film/Video Have students think of a recent movie they saw or describe the plot of a movie to students. Ask students to identify its climax and resolution. Is this resolution satisfying? Why or why not? Discuss and have students compare and contrast examples of satisfying movie, book, and television show endings.

Standards

National Theatre Standard: The student identifies and compares the various settings and reasons for creating dramas and attending theatre, film, television, and electronic media productions.

Reflect

Time: About 10 minutes

Assessment

▶ Have students evaluate their participation by completing the **Unit 1 Self-Criticism Questions** on page 32.

▶ Use the assessment rubric to evaluate the students' participation in the **Unit Activity** and to assess their understanding of plot.

▶ Have students complete the **Unit 1 Quick Quiz** on page 33.

	3 Points	2 Points	1 Point
Perception	Gives full attention to review. Has mastered an understanding of the occasional necessity of conflict in friendship.	Gives partial attention to review. Is developing an understanding of the occasional need for conflict in a friendship.	Gives little or no attention to review. Minimally understands the occasional necessity of conflict in friendship.
Creative Expression	Participates in the dramatization of a plot's section using all of the following: accuracy, creative interpretation, and appropriate language and actions.	Participates in the dramatization of a plot's section using three of the following: accuracy, creative interpretation, and appropriate language and actions.	Participates in the dramatization of a plot's section using two of the following: accuracy, creative interpretation, and appropriate language and actions.
History and Culture	Writes a paragraph clearly describing the plot of a story in which a risk was taken, including the risk a character took and the consequences of the risk. Accurately compares "Adventure in the Wild Wood" to the story he or she chose.	Writes a paragraph describing the plot clearly; does not include one of the following: the risk a character took or the consequences of the risk. Compares some but not all of the plot elements in "Adventure in the Wild Wood" to the story he or she chose.	Writes a paragraph describing some elements of the plot they chose; does not include the risk a character took and the consequences of the risk. Creates a poor comparison of "Adventure in the Wild Wood" and the story he or she chose.
Evaluation	Thoughtfully and honestly evaluates own participation using the four steps of art criticism.	Attempts to evaluate own participation, but shows an incomplete understanding of evaluation criteria.	Makes a minimal attempt to evaluate own participation.

Apply

▶ Ask students whether Mole's desire to see Badger created conflict between Mole and Rat. *(yes)* Say, "Do you think the risk Mole took was wise? Why or why not?" *(no, because he went alone to a dangerous place, and so on)*

▶ Tell students that Rat had to create conflict because his friend wanted to make a dangerous choice. Brainstorm with students dangerous or unwise risks they have seen people take and ways they could encourage them to not take those risks. *(not wearing seat belts, smoking; I can wear my seat belt. I can ask them not to smoke.)*

View a Performance

Plot in Storytelling

▶ Have students identify and discuss aspects of appropriate audience behavior. Remind them to watch the performance quietly; an audience's job is being respectful of the performers and other audience members.

▶ If you have the *Artsource*® videocassette or DVD, have students view "The Long-Haired Girl," a Chinese folktale told through dramatized storytelling by Eth-Noh-Tec. Alternatively, you may show students another storytelling recording.

▶ Discuss the performance with students using the following questions:

Describe Briefly retell the order of events. *(A girl finds spring water when she pulls out a turnip, the spirit-king of the mountain warns her not to tell anyone about it, and so on.)* Describe the people, fantastic creatures, and their relationships. *(The long-haired girl has a sick mother; the girl is kind and wants to help people, and so on.)*

Analyze What is the story's problem? *(The girl wants to tell people about the water, but the spirit-king will kill her if she does.)* What is the climax? *(When the girl is about to be killed, and the little green man saves her.)* What is the resolution? *(The girl's hair grows back and she returns home to her village.)*

Interpret Imagine you were going to make a play of this story. How would a play be similar to or different than your experience of this dramatized storytelling?

Decide What was the most exciting part of the plot?

> "Drama work involves a rich and situated sense of learning how to learn . . . This is part of the joy of drama; it is honest inquiry and we do not know what we will experience or learn when we begin."
>
> —Jeffrey D. Wilhelm, teacher

LEARN ABOUT CAREERS IN THEATRE

Explain to students that a playwright creates a play's plot and writes the lines actors will speak in the play. An important aspect of a playwright's job is to come up with an interesting plot that keeps the audience's attention and makes sense. A playwright may also suggest actions the actors could use onstage, although actors may not always follow these. Ask students to imagine they are a playwright who is writing a play version of a book they recently read as a class. Ask them what the main idea of the plot would be. Would the climax and resolution stay the same? Would students choose to change any of the elements of the plot? Why or why not?

Standards

National Theatre Standard: The student analyzes and explains personal preferences and constructs meanings from classroom dramatizations and from theatre, film, television, and electronic media productions.

Name _____ Date _____

Unit 1 Self-Criticism Questions

Think about how you acted out a scene from "Adventure in the Wild Wood." Then answer the questions below.

1. **Describe** What kinds of speech and actions did you use in the dramatization?

   _____
   _____
   _____

2. **Analyze** How did your speech and action help show the plot?

   _____
   _____
   _____

3. **Interpret** How is your life like or unlike the life of the character you played?

   _____
   _____
   _____

4. **Decide** Would you change anything about how you acted in the theatre activity?

   _____
   _____
   _____

Name _____ Date _____

Unit 1 Quick Quiz

Completely fill in the bubble of the best answer for each question below.

1. **Plot is**
   - Ⓐ a person in a story or drama.
   - Ⓑ the most exciting part of a story or drama.
   - Ⓒ the sequence of events in a story or drama.
   - Ⓓ an actor's speech.

2. **Climax is**
   - Ⓕ the beginning of a story or drama.
   - Ⓖ a problem in a story or drama.
   - Ⓗ the main plot of a story or drama.
   - Ⓙ the turning point of a story or drama.

3. **Resolution is**
   - Ⓐ the working out of problems at a story or drama's end.
   - Ⓑ the turning point of a story or drama.
   - Ⓒ the conflict in a story or drama.
   - Ⓓ the complication in a story or drama.

4. **Which of the following is *not* one of the five Ws?**
   - Ⓕ who
   - Ⓖ when
   - Ⓗ which
   - Ⓙ why

5. **A complication is**
   - Ⓐ something that makes the main problem easier to solve.
   - Ⓑ something that makes the main problem go away.
   - Ⓒ something that makes the main problem harder to solve.
   - Ⓓ none of the above.

Score _____ (Top Score 5)

UNIT 2 Character

Unit Overview

Lesson 1 • Characters Act and Feel A character's feelings and desires affect his or her actions. *Dramatic Movement*

Lesson 2 • Characters Relate Actors identify and show character relationships in a drama. *Tableau*

Lesson 3 • Characters Want Something A character's objective, or desire, in a scene gives him or her the motivation to act or speak. *Improvisation*

Lesson 4 • Action and Inaction A character's choices to act or not to act affect other characters and, ultimately, a story or drama's outcome. *Improvisation*

Lesson 5 • Characters Solve a Problem Characters solve problems in a story or play. *Dramatization*

Lesson 6 • Unit Activity: Scripted Monologue This activity will give students the opportunity to show character thoughts and feelings in a written monologue.

See pages T3–T20 for more about **Theatre Technique Tips.**

Introduce Unit Concepts

"Characters are people and sometimes animals or objects with human characteristics in stories and dramas. Actors bring characters to life."

"Los personajes son personas y a veces animales u objetos con características humanas en historias o dramas. Los actores dan vida a los personajes."

Character

▶ Explain that a character is a person in a story or play. A character can also be an animal or an object with human characteristics.

▶ Tell students that most characters want something. Ask students to think of an important character from a movie. Discuss what the character's major desires were.

Vocabulary

Discuss the following vocabulary words.

character personaje—a person in a novel, play, or poem

motivation motivación—the reason a character acts or speaks

objective objetivo—the goal a character works toward in a certain scene; part of the character's major goal for the entire play

Unit Links

Visual Arts: Shape, Pattern, Rhythm, and Movement

▶ Compare and contrast the ways emotions are expressed in theatre and in art. Discuss the ways actors in formal and informal theatre show a character's feelings through movements, speech, facial expressions, and gestures. Even though most paintings and photographs do not move or speak, artists can use repeated and changing shapes to create a feeling of movement and to communicate feelings.

▶ Show students the image of a painting with examples of shapes and pattern, such as *Composition* by Stuart Davis. What feelings do the shapes and patterns create? *(playfulness, happiness)* Have students pantomime characters whose walks are motivated by these feelings.

Reading Theme: Dollars and Sense

▶ Ask, "Why do most people have jobs or own businesses?" *(They need to earn money.)* Can a desire for money cause problems? *(Yes, because sometimes people steal or hurt others to get it.)*

▶ Discuss with students different types of jobs or work done by characters from books, movies, television programs, or plays. *(Pa in* Little House in the Big Woods *grows or hunts most of their food; Henry Huggins works to prove he can handle a paper route in* Henry and the Paper Route, *and so on.)*

Teacher Background

Background on Character

A character is a person or a personified animal or object in a play, story, or literary work. In a play, a character has a central desire, or super-objective, that can be broken down into smaller objectives in each scene. The character's motivation for action, inaction, and speech flows out of these objectives. In theatre, actors analyze and investigate these motivations and objectives in order to portray characters.

Background on Acting

Not all actors portray characters in the same way. Actors can focus on a character's movements, behavior, or feelings. Some actors try to experience a character's feelings so as to understand why he or she acts and speaks in a particular way; some actors use experiences from their own life to help them understand a character. This unit explores ways actors reveal a character to their audience.

Research in Theatre Education

"This study reports several significant results. One is that children are more engaged during dramatizations than when just listening. Another is that several key ingredients of story understanding are better conveyed through drama: main idea, character identification, and character motivation. These are essential elements of comprehension."

—James S. Catterall

on "Children's Story Comprehension as a Result of Storytelling and Story Dramatization: A Study of the Child as Spectator and as Participant in *Critical Links*

Differentiated Instruction

Reteach
Have students choose a character from their favorite movie and describe his or her actions. Ask them to choose one of these actions and use it to infer motivation.

Challenge
Have students create a motivation for a character, such as not wanting to go to a party. Then have them perform a short pantomime in which the character performs an everyday task related to and affected by the motivation.

Special Needs
Have students name an emotion they are feeling. How do they show this emotion to others? Show pictures of people experiencing emotions. Discuss how each person shows his or her emotion.

Theatre's Effects Across the Curriculum

★ **Reading/Writing**
Reading Response Reading a story and then portraying a character from the story gives students another way to practice interpreting a written text.

★ **Math**
Problem Solving Students can solve a problem by dramatizing a character's problem and exploring possible solutions.

★ **Science**
Observation In scientific investigations and in character studies, students observe and gather information to use in making predictions.

★ **Social Studies**
Citizenship Identifying and discussing character traits can help students more easily identify the character traits of effective leaders and productive citizens.

★ **Music**
Character Traits Music can stimulate emotional states and enhance positive character traits such as courage and loyalty while making theatrical presentations more powerful.

★ **Dance**
Dramatizing Problems When students identify and dramatize a character's problem, they better understand that problem and can explore it in dance through the use of rhythm, energy, and space.

Objectives

Perception To identify ways characters' feelings affect their actions

Creative Expression To show character motivations using dramatic movement

History and Culture To learn about stock characters

Evaluation To informally evaluate one's own work

Materials
- Copies of **"Characters Act and Feel" Warm-Up,** p. 37
- Journals or writing paper

Vocabulary
character
motivation

Standards

National Theatre Standard: The student is expected to select movement, music, or visual elements to enhance the mood of a classroom dramatization.

Listening/Speaking Standard: The student uses eye contact and gestures that engage the audience.

Science Standard: The student analyzes and interprets information to construct reasonable explanations from direct and indirect evidence.

Lesson 1: Characters Act and Feel

Focus
Time: About 10 minutes

"In this lesson we will use dramatic movement to show character motivations." *(See page T13 for more about Dramatic Movement.)*

Activate Prior Knowledge

▶ Distribute the **"Characters Act and Feel" Warm-Up** and have students read the fable.

▶ Explain that a character's motivation is the reason he or she acts and speaks. Discuss the milkmaid's motivations for actions such as talking to herself. *(She was excited about her dreams for the future.)*

Teach
Time: About 15 minutes

Prepare Divide students into groups. Have students create a space.

Lead Say, "I will assign one action, such as setting the table, to each group. I will assign each group member a different motivation. Each group member will let the motivation affect the action."

▶ To model this, pantomime a character setting a dinner table very carefully so that everything will look perfect for his or her guest.

▶ Assign one everyday action, such as cleaning up a room, to each group; assign a different motivation, such as trying not to wake a baby, to each group member. Remind them to use safe body movements. Have each group member perform his or her action for the class.

Informal Assessment Did each student perform the action in a way that demonstrated the motivation?

History and Culture

Tell students a stock character is a character whose feelings and actions come from cultural stereotypes—oversimplified ideas shared by a group of people. The mad scientist, the damsel in distress, and the sidekick are all examples of stock characters. Many American stock characters come from the ancient Greek and Roman theatre.

Reflect
Time: About 5 minutes

▶ Have students describe each of their characters, and have them compare and contrast the different ways the same action was performed due to different motivations.

Apply

Journal: Describing
Have students write journal entries describing a time when a strong emotion caused them to act in a certain way.

Unit 2 • **Character**

Characters Act and Feel

The Milkmaid and her Pail
from *Aesop's Fables*

A farmer's daughter finished milking the cows and was carrying her pail of milk upon her head. As she walked along, she started to daydream, saying, "The milk in this pail will give me cream. I will make the cream into butter and take it to the market to sell. With the money, I will buy some eggs, and these will hatch into chickens. Then I'll sell some of the chickens, and with the money I'll buy myself a beautiful new dress, which I will wear to the dance. All the young men will admire me and want to dance with me, but I'll just toss my head and have nothing to say to them." At this, she forgot all about the pail on her head, and imagining herself at the dance, she tossed her head. Down went the pail, the milk spilled out all over the ground, and all her fine plans vanished in a moment!

Moral: Do not count your chickens before they are hatched.

Objectives

 Perception To identify ways characters relate

 Creative Expression To create a tableau showing character relationships

 History and Culture To learn about the origins of Japanese tableaux

Evaluation To informally evaluate one's own work

Materials

- Copies of **"Characters Relate" Warm-Up,** p. 39
- Journals or writing paper

Vocabulary

tableau

Unit Links

Visual Arts: Shape
Relationships can be shown visually in art, theatre, and dance. Tell students that when actors create tableaux, they arrange their bodies in ways that can visually show relationships. In a similar way, artists indicate relationships when they arrange shapes representing people in two-dimensional artwork. Have students compare and contrast the way relationships are visually shown in art, dance, and formal and informal theatre.

National Theatre Standard: The student collaborates to select interrelated characters, environments, and situations for classroom dramatizations.

Listening/Speaking Standard: The student interacts with peers in a variety of situations to develop and present familiar ideas (for example, conversations, whole group interactions, discussions).

Fine Arts Standard: The student expresses ideas through original artwork, using a variety of media with appropriate skill. The student is expected to integrate a variety of ideas about self, life events, family, and community in original artwork.

Lesson 2: Characters Relate

Focus
Time: About 10 minutes

"In this lesson we will use our bodies to create tableaux that show character relationships." *(See page T7 for more about Tableau.)*

Activate Prior Knowledge

▶ Distribute the **"Characters Relate" Warm-Up** and have students read the story.

▶ Discuss the social, emotional, and physical relationships of the merchant, the beggar, and the judge. *(The merchant has a higher social status than the beggar; the merchant treats the beggar badly; and so on.)* Did the judge act wisely? *(Yes, because he saw through the merchant's lie.)*

Teach
Time: About 15 minutes

Prepare Divide students into groups of three.

Lead Say, "Imagine you had a camera and were watching the action from 'The Bag of Gold.' What snapshot would you take to show these characters' relationships?"

▶ Have group members choose to be the beggar, the merchant, and the judge. Have each group decide what their snapshot will be. Remind them that they can be frozen in the process of speaking or acting.

▶ One at a time, have each group form its tableau when you make the camera sound, "Click"; instruct other groups to walk around silently and view it.

Informal Assessment Did each group's tableau illustrate character relationships?

 History and Culture

Tell students that in sixteenth-century Japan, tableaux were used in parades to show scenes from legends or the lives of old heroes. Have student groups choose one of their heroes and create a living "statue" of him or her in the act of doing what he or she is noted for.

Reflect
Time: About 5 minutes

▶ Discuss how students used their bodies to show who each character was, as well as his or her feelings, actions, and relationships.

Apply

Journal: Comparing and Contrasting
Tell students to think about a scene from their favorite movies. Have each student draw two sketches in their journals—one depicting the characters in the scene and one depicting a "snapshot" from the activity—and compare and contrast the relationships.

Characters Relate

The Bag of Gold
a Jewish folktale

A beggar found a leather bag that someone had dropped in the marketplace. When he opened it, he found 100 pieces of gold.

From somewhere in the marketplace he heard someone shout, "A reward! A reward to the one who finds my leather money bag!" It was a rich merchant.

The honest beggar came forward and gave the purse to the merchant. "Here is your money bag," he said. "May I have the reward?"

"Reward?" scoffed the merchant, greedily counting his gold. "Why my bag had 200 pieces of gold in it. Clearly you've stolen 100 pieces already—what more do you want?"

"I have not stolen anything," protested the beggar. "Let us take this matter before a judge."

The beggar and the merchant each told his side of the story. The judge listened carefully, and then she said, "I think you are both telling the truth. Here is my judgment: Merchant, you say that your lost bag held 200 gold pieces? That is a great deal of money. But the bag this beggar found had only 100 pieces of gold. Therefore, it cannot belong to you."

And with that the judge gave the purse and all the gold to the honest beggar.

Objectives

 **Perception** To identify a character's objective and motivation in a scripted scene

Creative Expression To improvise a conversation in which characters are motivated by opposing objectives while physicalizing the conflict

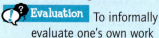 **History and Culture** To identify an objective of a historical figure

Evaluation To informally evaluate one's own work

Materials

- Copies of **"Characters Want Something" Warm-Up,** p. 41
- Journals or writing paper

Vocabulary

objective
motivation

Standards

National Theatre Standard: The student is expected to identify and compare similar characters and situations in stories and dramas from and about various cultures, illustrate with classroom dramatizations, and discuss how theatre reflects life.

Listening/Speaking Standard: The student prepares and gives presentations for specific occasions, audiences, and purposes (including but not limited to group discussions, informational or dramatic presentations).

Social Studies/History Standard: The student is expected to identify the accomplishments of significant explorers, such as Cabeza de Vaca, Christopher Columbus, Francisco Coronado, René Robert Cavelier, and Sieur de la Salle.

Lesson 3: Characters Want Something

Focus
Time: About 10 minutes

"In this lesson we will use improvisation to explore characters with opposing objectives." *(See page T4 for more about Improvisation.)*

Activate Prior Knowledge

▶ Distribute the **"Characters Want Something" Warm-Up.** Have students form pairs, read the scene aloud, and answer the questions.

▶ Say, "In theatre, character goals are called objectives; they give characters motivation for speech or action. Omar's objective is to get a bike. What actions are motivated by this objective?" *(He asks for a bike.)*

Teach
Time: About 15 minutes

Prepare Divide students into pairs.

Lead Tell students the conversation should focus on one character telling another about something he or she wants, while the other character has a conflicting objective that gets in the way. While they have the conversation, students should pantomime playing tug-of-war, pulling when they pursue their objective and resisting the other's pull.

▶ Give students a few minutes to come up with an appropriate situation. Allow them to adapt a situation from literature or history.

▶ Have students perform their improvisations for the class. Have students suggest ways the characters could resolve their conflict.

Informal Assessment Did each presentation reveal the characters' goals?

History and Culture

Explain to students that they can identify objectives of historical figures such as Sieur de la Salle, a French explorer, who sailed to the New World in 1684. Although his king wanted him to travel to the Rio Grande, la Salle wanted to start a colony in the Mississippi River Valley. La Salle got lost, however, and landed near what is now Houston, Texas. What was la Salle's objective? *(start a colony)* What actions were motivated by this objective? *(He tricked the king; he tried to sail there.)*

Reflect
Time: About 5 minutes

▶ Discuss how character objectives motivated their speech.

Apply

Journal: Explaining
Have students write journal entries describing a time in their lives when they had an important reason to save money. Did their important reason, or objective, give them the motivation they needed?

Name _____ Date _____

Characters Want Something

Read the dialogue below, and then answer the questions.

OMAR: Mom, you know I have always wanted a mountain bike.

MOM: I know, but I told you that you have to come up with half the money in order to get the bike.

OMAR: But Mom, I'm only ten. I can't get a *real* job!

MOM: There are plenty of ways for you to earn money. You can cut grass, walk dogs, or help with chores.

OMAR: Why does it have to be so hard?

MOM: If you really want the bike, you'll work to get it.

1. What does Omar want?

_____

_____

_____

2. In the script above, how is Omar trying to get what he wants?

_____

_____

_____

3. Do you think he will do what his mom says?

_____

_____

_____

Objectives

 Perception To identify character action and inaction

 Creative Expression To perform an improvisation exploring a historical character's actions and inactions

 History and Culture To consider ways the Civil War affected Native Americans

 Evaluation To informally evaluate one's own work

Materials

- Copies of **"Action and Inaction" Warm-Up**, p. 43
- Journals or writing paper

Unit Links

Visual Arts: Rhythm and Movement
Compare and contrast the way rhythm can communicate ideas and emotions in art, theatre, and music. Tell students artists use visual rhythm, or repeated shapes and colors, to move viewers' eyes across artwork. Actors in formal and informal theatre can create rhythmic character actions, such as sword fighting or dancing. Discuss examples of rhythm from music with which students are familiar.

Standards

National Theatre Standard: The student is expected to assume roles that exhibit concentration and contribute to the action of classroom dramatizations based on personal experience and heritage, imagination, literature, and history.

Listening/Speaking Standard: The student delivers brief recitations and oral presentations about familiar experiences or interests that are organized around a coherent thesis statement.

Social Studies Standard: The student understands the political, economic, and social changes in Texas during the last half of the nineteenth century.

Lesson 4: Action and Inaction

Focus
Time: About 10 minutes

"In this lesson we will improvise an interview to explore character actions and inactions." *(See page T4 for more about Improvisation.)*

Activate Prior Knowledge

▶ Distribute the **"Action and Inaction" Warm-Up** and have students read the piece.

▶ Discuss the actions of Colonel Carleton, the California scouts, and the Texas Confederates.

Teach
Time: About 15 minutes

Prepare Divide students into three groups.

Lead Explain that a character's actions result from thoughts and feelings. Choices of action or inaction affect other characters.

▶ Assign each group one of the following: Colonel Carleton, a scout from the California Column, or a Texas Confederate soldier. Members should take turns answering questions as the character and asking questions as reporters; each member should ask and answer at least one question. They should plan to ask questions about plans for action, actions taken, and actions he or she did not take.

▶ Allow a few minutes to plan, telling them it is okay to make imaginative, educated guesses. Have each group improvise its interview for the class.

Informal Assessment Did each group use the historical information to ask questions or improvise a character?

 History and Culture

Tell students many people forget that the Civil War affected Native Americans. Some Native Americans fought in the war; others saw it as a chance to take back some of their land. If time allows, have one student group research actions of a local or regional Native American tribe during the Civil War, and have another investigate the tribe's dance or theatre traditions. Have groups share their findings.

Reflect
Time: About 5 minutes

▶ Discuss any invented reasons groups suggested for character action and inaction. Which seem most likely based on the historical passage?

Apply

Journal: Describing and Inferring
Tell students that the government of California sent shipments of gold to help the Union effort. In their journals, have students describe the effect of a time they shared money to help someone and how inaction would have changed the outcome.

Action and Inaction

The Battle of Picacho Pass

In 1862, Picacho Pass was far from the major battles of the Civil War. The tall, rocky pieces of this dead volcano stood in the Sonaran Desert of Arizona. The closest settlement, a small town named Tucson, was 50 miles away.

The Civil War did affect this area, however. The Texas Confederate Army was on its way, hoping to control some important trails in the area. Soon it was in the town of Tucson. The California Union Army heard about this and formed a group of volunteers called the California Column. The leader of the column was Colonel James Carleton.

Carleton and the California Column marched into Arizona. They had been warned not to use the old Gila Trail because there was not enough water for so many men, but Carleton was smart. He split his troops into two groups so they needed less water and could still use the trail.

A group of scouts left the Column, planning to check out Tucson. Because they were worried about an ambush, they split into two groups when they came to Picacho Pass. Early in the afternoon the Texas Confederate Army attacked. The fighting went on for several hours until the Californian scouts retreated in the late afternoon.

But when the California Column came to Tucson, the Texas Confederate soldiers were gone. Lacking supplies and soldiers, they had retreated, and the California Column did not have to fight them again. The battle fought between the scouts and the Confederates became known as the Battle of Picacho Pass; it is known for being the westernmost battle fought during the Civil War.

Objectives

Perception To identify problems faced by certain characters

Creative Expression To explore the way characters solve a problem through dramatization

History and Culture To compare radio and television news

Evaluation To informally evaluate one's own work

Materials

○ Journals or writing paper

Standards

National Theatre Standard: The student understands context by recognizing the role of theatre, film, television, and electronic media in daily life.

Listening/Speaking Standard: The student responds to speakers by asking questions, making contributions, and paraphrasing what is said.

Language Arts Standard: The student analyzes the characteristics of various types of texts (genres).

44

Lesson 5: Characters Solve a Problem

Focus
Time: About 10 minutes

"In this lesson we will invent and dramatize the outcome of some unsolved problems." *(See page T6 for more about Dramatization.)*

Activate Prior Knowledge
▶ Read aloud **"The Golden Goose."**

▶ Discuss some of the problems characters encounter in the story. Explain that a main character usually faces a problem; the more difficult this problem is to solve, the more interesting the play is.

Teach
Time: About 10 minutes

Prepare Divide students into small groups.

Lead Say, "Dummling solved the princess's problem. Whose problems were not solved at the story's end? *(The other people stuck to the goose.)* What happened to those people? Did they remain stuck?"

▶ Tell students each group will create a nightly news report explaining the logical sequence of events that happened to these people the week after the story's end. Remind them to focus on the characters' problem and how it is solved.

▶ Allow time for planning. Encourage them to have news anchors, "on-the-scene" reporters, and subjects to be interviewed. Have each group share its nightly news story.

Informal Assessment Did members of each group dramatize one potential outcome of a problem?

History and Culture

Ask students how different life was for Americans before they had radio or television news. *(They didn't find out about things for a long time; they couldn't get or give help fast.)* Discuss with students some strengths and weaknesses of radio and television news and entertainment. *(You can't see anything on the radio, and so on.)*

Reflect
Time: About 5 minutes

▶ Discuss with students some behavior differences between audience members watching real news reports and audience members watching a live drama. *(Television viewers can change the channel or talk and so on.)*

Apply

Journal: Describing
In their journals, have students describe a movie or television show in which the main character had a problem that seemed impossible to solve and how it was resolved.

Unit 2 • **Character**

The Golden Goose

from *Grimm's Fairy Tales* by the Brothers Grimm (Adapted)

There was a man who had three sons, the youngest of whom was called Dummling. One day Dummling wanted to cut some wood, so he packed himself a lunch and set off for the forest.

When he came to the forest, he saw a little gray man. "Good day," the man said. "Will you give me something to eat and drink?"

"I have only bread and water," Dummling said, "but if you like, you and I may share it." So they sat down. When Dummling pulled out his ash cake, it had become a fine sweet cake, and instead of water, he had cold milk.

"You have a good heart," the gray man said, "so I will tell you a secret. Cut down that old tree over there and you will find something at the roots." Then the little man walked down the road.

Dummling went and cut down the tree, and when it fell there was a goose with feathers of pure gold sitting in the roots. He lifted her and carried her out of the forest.

Soon he came to an inn. The innkeeper had three daughters, and when they saw the golden goose, they decided they must have one of its feathers. The eldest daughter snuck up behind Dummling, but when she touched the goose, her hand stuck fast. The second sister tried to help, but soon she too was stuck. And so it was with the third. Dummling went on his way, not paying the girls any attention. They had to run after him, now left, now right, wherever his legs took him.

In the middle of some fields a parson saw them and thought, "Young girls should not chase young men!" He went to lead the youngest girl away, but no sooner did he touch her than he was stuck fast to her hand.

Before long the parson's assistant came by and saw the parson running behind three girls. He called out, "Don't forget— you have a wedding to perform today." He ran and took the parson by the sleeve, and was stuck fast as well.

Two men digging in a field saw this odd group going down the road. They went to help free the parson, but no sooner did they touch him than they stuck fast. All seven of them had to run behind Dummling and the goose.

Soon Dummling came to a city. The king who ruled this city had a daughter who had never laughed. He had made a decree that any man who could make her laugh should marry her. When Dummling heard this, he went with his goose and all her train before the king's daughter.

As soon as the princess saw the seven people running on and on, one behind the other, she began to laugh and laugh, and she kept on laughing as if she would never stop. So Dummling married her, and she has not gone a day without laughing ever since.

But no one knows what became of the golden goose and all those who were stuck to it.

Objectives

 Perception To review ways that actors portray characters and to connect the concept of character motivation to real life

 Creative Expression To write and perform a character monologue based on a character in "The Barber's Clever Wife"

 History and Culture To research the environment, cultures, and theatre of India

 Evaluation To thoughtfully and honestly evaluate one's own participation using the four steps of criticism

Materials

- Copies of **"The Barber's Clever Wife,"** pp. 127–129
- Copies of the **Unit 2 Self-Criticism Questions,** p. 50
- Copies of the **Unit 2 Quick Quiz,** p. 51
- ○ *Artsource®* **Performing Arts Resource Package** (optional)

Standards

National Theatre Standard: The student understands context by recognizing the role of theatre, film, television, and electronic media in daily life. The student is expected to identify and compare similar characters and situations in stories and dramas from and about various cultures, illustrate with classroom dramatizations, and discuss how theatre reflects life.

46

Unit Activity: Scripted Monologue

Focus

Time: About 10 minutes

Review Unit Concepts

"A character is a person, or sometimes an animal or object with human characteristics, in a play, literary work, movie, or story. Characters' actions result from their feelings, thoughts, and objectives. Their actions and inactions affect characters with whom they have relationships. The main character in a story or play works hard to solve a central problem."

"Un personaje es una persona, o a veces un animal u objeto con caraterísticas humanas, en un drama, una obra literaria, una película o una historia. Las acciones de los personajes resultan de sus sentimientos, pensamientos y objetivos. Sus acciones y faltas de acción afectan a los personajes con quienes tienen relaciones. El personaje principal en una historia o drama trabaja duro para resolver un problema central."

▶ Review with students the different elements of character they dramatized in this unit.

▶ Review the unit vocabulary on page 34.

 ### History and Culture

Remind students that "The Barber's Clever Wife" is a traditional story from India. Tell them characters are affected by their cultures; for example, a man or woman in another culture or time period might move or speak differently than men or women in our own culture. Have one group of students research some cultural groups in India; have another group research some types of theatre performed in India. Allow them to use the Internet if possible. Have groups share their research with the class. How would this information change the way students perform their monologues?

Classroom Management Tips

The following are tips for managing your classroom during the **Rehearsals** and **Activity:**

✔ **Give Prompts** During the **First Rehearsal,** if students copy other students' "thoughts" for a character or cannot think of what to say, prompt them with questions relevant to their scene, such as, "How are you feeling, Manisha?" or "Are you trying to get something right now?"

✔ **Encourage Creativity** Tell pairs they may add events to the story and reference them in their monologues. Encourage them not to be afraid to add dimension and personality to the characters of the robber, Manisha, and Alok.

Unit 2 • **Character**

Teach

Time: Two 15-minute rehearsal periods
One 15-minute activity period

First Rehearsal

▶ Distribute copies of **"The Barber's Clever Wife"** on pages 127–129.

▶ Discuss the characters and their relationships in the story. How does Manisha feel about Alok? How do the robbers feel about Manisha? Do these feelings change throughout the story?

▶ Divide students into groups of nine, and tell them they are going to create a tableau to illustrate two scenes in the story. Manisha, Alok, and the seven robbers should be present in at least one of the scenes.

▶ Allow two minutes for planning, and then have one group create its tableau. Say, "I wonder what each character is thinking right now? I have an invisible microphone. When I hold that microphone in front of each character, he or she will speak his or her thoughts." Hold the microphone alternately in front of several characters. Repeat with each group.

Second Rehearsal

▶ Ask, "Who is the main character in this story? *(Manisha)* What are some of her objectives from different parts of the story? *(She wants to plow the field, she wants to escape, and so on.)* What action does she take that is motivated by these objectives?" *(She tricks the robbers.)* Repeat these questions for the character of Alok.

▶ Divide students into pairs. Have each pair choose the character of Manisha, Alok, or a robber. Explain to students that each pair will work together to plan and write a monologue for their character; a monologue is a long speech spoken by one character. The character may speak directly to the audience or may be speaking to another character. Tell them to incorporate elements from their research in the **History and Culture** section.

▶ Say, "Imagine how your character feels after the end of the story. How does he or she feel about the other characters? Pretend he or she is speaking to a friend, and invent a motivation for the character to explain what happened in the story." Remind them to write in the first person. *(See page T10 for more about Script Writing.)*

▶ Have pairs write their monologues. Encourage them to perform readings for each other and use the readings to make revisions.

Character Activity

▶ Have students get back in their pairs. Tell them to make any final changes to their monologues.

▶ Have each student perform his or her monologue for the class. Remind them to speak and move in ways their characters would. Have the class identify appropriate audience behavior and agree to apply it.

▶ Discuss the different thoughts and ideas students gave to the same characters.

Standards

National Theatre Standard: The student writes scripts by planning and recording improvisations based on personal experience and heritage, imagination, literature, and history. The student is expected to improvise dialogue to tell stories and formalize improvisations by writing or recording the dialogue.

Lesson 6 • Unit Activity

Unit Links

Visual Arts: Pattern
Visual artists, musical composers, dance choreographers, actors in informal playmaking, and playwrights in formal playmaking can use aspects of pattern. Tell students that patterns are repeated shapes, or motifs, in two-dimensional artwork. Remind students that a story can have a sequence of repeated events or actions. Ask students to identify a pattern of events in "The Barber's Clever Wife." *(Manisha keeps tricking the robbers in different ways; Manisha keeps coming up with clever solutions to problems.)* Compare and contrast the ways dance, music, theatre, and art use pattern to communicate ideas and emotions.

Theatrical Arts Connection

Television Discuss a popular television show that students are familiar with in which a husband and wife relate. Describe an episode from the show. Does one character seem cleverer than the other? Have students compare and contrast this relationship with Manisha and Alok's relationship in "The Barber's Clever Wife."

Film Show a clip from a movie or have students suggest a character from a movie they have seen. Discuss the character's actions and reactions to problems he or she encounters. Compare and contrast film and live theatre, and discuss the role of each in American society.

Standards

National Theatre Standard: The student understands context by recognizing the role of theatre, film, television, and electronic media in daily life.

Reflect

Time: About 10 minutes

Assessment

▶ Have students evaluate their participation by completing the **Unit 2 Self-Criticism Questions** on page 50.

▶ Use the assessment rubric to evaluate the students' participation in the **Unit Activity** and to assess their understanding of character.

▶ Have students complete the **Unit 2 Quick Quiz** on page 51.

	3 Points	2 Points	1 Point
Perception	Gives full attention to review. Masters an understanding of the concept of motivations and problems in real life.	Gives partial attention to review. Is developing an understanding of the concept of motivations and problems in real life.	Gives little or no attention to review. Has minimal understanding of the concept of motivations and problems in real life.
Creative Expression	Writes a monologue that portrays several of a character's thoughts and feelings about the story's events. Performs this monologue using appropriate facial expressions, gestures, and tone of voice.	Writes a monologue that portrays some of a character's thoughts and feelings about the story's events. Performs this monologue using some facial expressions, gestures, and tone of voice.	Writes a monologue that poorly portrays a character's thoughts and feelings. Performs this monologue using only one of the following: appropriate facial expressions, gestures, and tone of voice.
History and Culture	Fully participates in researching either a culture of India or an Indian theatre style. Fully relates this information to the monologue.	Shows some participation in researching either a culture of India or an Indian theatre style. Relates two aspects of this information to the monologue.	Poorly participates in researching either a culture of India or an Indian theatre style. Has trouble relating any of this information to the monologue.
Evaluation	Thoughtfully and honestly evaluates own participation using the four steps of art criticism.	Attempts to evaluate own participation, but shows an incomplete understanding of evaluation criteria.	Makes a minimal attempt to evaluate own participation.

Apply

▶ Discuss the problems that Manisha faced in the story, and have students compare and contrast these problems to problems in their own lives.

▶ Say, "The robbers were motivated by greed and revenge. Can you think of anyone now or from history whose main motivation in life related to helping others rather than hurting them?" *(Martin Luther King Jr., my mother, and so on)* Discuss ways this person chose to work for others rather than to make money for himself or herself.

View a Performance

Character in Dance

▶ Have students identify and discuss aspects of appropriate audience behavior. Remind them to watch the performance quietly; an audience's job is being respectful of the performers and other audience members.

▶ If you have the ***Artsource*** videocassette or DVD, have students view "Waltz of the Flowers" from *The Nutcracker* performed by the Joffrey Ballet of Chicago. Alternatively, you may show students another ballet with distinct characters.

▶ Discuss the performance with students using the following questions:

Describe What types of movements did the dancers use? *(light, twirling movements)* Describe their costumes and the backdrop behind them. *(purple, floating costumes, images of trees)*

Analyze What characters did the dancers portray? *(flowers)* How did the dancers' movements help create these characters? *(They moved lightly, as if they were flowers swaying and floating in the air, and so on.)*

Interpret Compare and contrast the dancers' movements with the movements you used when performing your monologue.

Decide What other types of personified objects would you like to see ballet dancers portray? How do you think they might do that?

LEARN ABOUT CAREERS IN THEATRE

Ask students to share ways an actor tells the audience about a character. *(words, movements, facial expressions)* Explain to students that an actor's job is to tell a story through the eyes of his or her character. The actor must show the audience who the character is and what his or her motivations are. Even actors who play small parts, such as one of the many robbers, can make these characters seem more real by giving them individual personalities and styles of movement. Ask students to imagine they are an actor portraying one of the robbers from "The Barber's Clever Wife." How could they set their character apart from the others? *(I could be louder than everyone; I could have a different motivation than the other robbers, and so on.)* Have students compare and contrast the ways actors and playwrights create characters.

"You can throw away the privilege of acting, but that would be such a shame. The tribe has elected you to tell its story. You are the shaman/healer, that's what the storyteller is, and I think it's important for actors to appreciate that."

—Ben Kingsley (1943–), actor

Standards

National Theatre Standard: The student articulates emotional responses to and explains personal preferences about the whole as well as parts of dramatic performances.

Name _____ Date _____

Unit 2 — Self-Criticism Questions

Think about your performance of your character monologue from "The Barber's Clever Wife." Then answer the questions below.

1. **Describe** What kinds of thoughts and feelings did your character have? How did you use your body to show these thoughts and feelings when you performed the monologue?

   _____
   _____
   _____
   _____

2. **Analyze** What was your character's motivation to speak this monologue?

   _____
   _____
   _____
   _____

3. **Interpret** How are you like or unlike this character?

   _____
   _____
   _____
   _____

4. **Decide** Would you change anything about how you wrote or performed your monologue?

   _____
   _____
   _____
   _____

Name _____ Date _____

Unit 2 Quick Quiz

Completely fill in the bubble of the best answer for each question below.

1. **A character is**
   - Ⓐ not played by an actor in a play.
   - Ⓑ a person or a personified animal or object in a play or story.
   - Ⓒ a feeling someone has that makes him or her act.
   - Ⓓ the person who writes a play.

2. **A character's objective is**
   - Ⓕ his or her goal in a certain scene.
   - Ⓖ the high point of a play.
   - Ⓗ not something that leads to action.
   - Ⓙ his or her secret that is told in a play.

3. **A reason a character speaks or acts is called a**
   - Ⓐ dialogue.
   - Ⓑ resolution.
   - Ⓒ monologue.
   - Ⓓ motivation.

4. **A character's actions can show**
   - Ⓕ who the character is.
   - Ⓖ how the character feels.
   - Ⓗ how the character feels about other characters.
   - Ⓙ all of the above.

5. **Which of the following is *not* true?**
   - Ⓐ A monologue is a speech spoken by one character.
   - Ⓑ Characters solve problems.
   - Ⓒ Characters never act because they want something.
   - Ⓓ Characters are often created by playwrights.

Score _____ (Top Score 5)

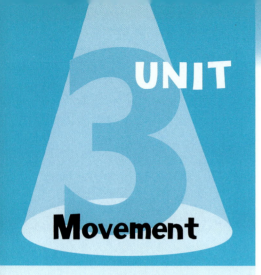

UNIT 3 Movement

Unit Overview

Lesson 1 • Movement Snapshots Creating a character snapshot can show character relationships and feelings. *Tableau*

Lesson 2 • Movement and the Five Ws Character movement can show many of the five *W*s. *Dramatic Movement*

Lesson 3 • Shapes in Movement Actors sometimes use creative, dance-like movements. *Creative Movement*

Lesson 4 • Rhythm and Repetition Repeated movement created in an orderly pattern can create a feeling of energy. *Dramatic Movement*

Lesson 5 • Action and Reaction Characters physically act and react to each other. *Pantomime*

Lesson 6 • Unit Activity: Dramatized Literary Selection This activity will give students the opportunity to show elements of movement in a dramatized story.

See pages T3–T20 for more about **Theatre Technique Tips.**

Introduce Unit Concepts

"Movement is important in dramatic activities. Actors use character movement to reveal a character's mood, feelings, or physical state."
"Movimiento es importante para las actividades dramáticas. Actores usan movimiento como personaje para revelar el humor, los sentimientos o el estado físico de un personaje."

Movement

▶ Discuss students' observations of people's movement. Explain that actors often use observations of human movement when developing characters.

▶ Compare and contrast the movement of actors in formal and informal theatre with the movement of dancers. Explain that actors sometimes use movement that is similar to dance to communicate ideas or to personify invisible forces, such as the wind.

Vocabulary

Discuss the following vocabulary words.

rhythm *ritmo*—in terms of movement, an orderly or irregular pattern of movements

repetition *repeticón*—in terms of movement, a pattern of repeated movements

Unit Links

Visual Arts: Color and Value
▶ Discuss with students ways that an actor's movements can communicate ideas and feelings, such as a slow walk communicating weariness or sadness. An artist can communicate ideas and feelings using elements such as color and value, a color's degree of lightness or darkness. Have students discuss colors that evoke feelings. Have each student choose a color and move around the room in a way that expresses that color. Have them describe how that color would feel, move, and sound.

▶ Show students the image of a colorful painting, such as *Pas de Deux* by Miriam Shapiro. Discuss how color creates a feeling of excitement and movement. Have students select music that creates the same mood as the painting; have them use the music and the image to help them select movement that the characters from the painting might use.

Reading Theme: From Mystery to Medicine
▶ Ask students to think of times when they were sick. How did they feel? Discuss how a character's movements can show feelings.

▶ Discuss what it would be like if there were no medicines. Explain that people through time have learned more and more about ways to help sick people.

Teacher Background

Background on Movement
Many actors carefully train their bodies to increase their strength and range of motion. A director often plans actors' movements onstage, called blocking, taking into account the needs of the audience. Blocking may be developed before rehearsals begin or after actors have worked on improvised movements. Blocking may also change based on actors' ideas; actors create many of the gestures and movements within this blocking. In a musical, the actors' dance movements are planned by a choreographer.

Background on Acting
Movement helps show a character's inner feelings and outer characteristics, such as emotions, age, or physical state. Movement can also show the audience what is happening in a character's environment, such as weather conditions. Actors use different movements to portray different character traits.

Research in Theatre Education
" . . . [In this study,] the surprising result that enacting a text makes a new text more comprehensible is interpreted as demonstration of the power of drama to develop text comprehension skills that transfer to new material."

—Terry L. Baker
on "Strengthening Verbal Skills Through the Use of Classroom Drama: A Clear Link" in *Critical Links*

Differentiated Instruction

Reteach
Have students choose a character from a book the class recently read. Have volunteers list five of this character's traits and move in a way to communicate these traits; have other students guess the traits that each actor's movements communicate.

Challenge
Have students imagine and create a character, including details such as age and personality. Then have them act out the character's movements and have other students describe the character.

Special Needs
Students with disabilities who express reticence in participating in movement or other pantomime activities can be encouraged by providing plenty of time for guided practice of selected skills.

Theatre's Effects Across the Curriculum

★ **Reading/Writing**
Writing Comprehension Journal writing gives students the opportunity to express, discover, record, develop, and reflect ideas.

★ **Math**
Patterns and Relationships Student exploration of kinesthetic rhythms and repetitive movements can help them better understand number patterns.

★ **Science**
Cause and Effect By dramatizing historical events, students learn how past events affect events in the present and future.

★ **Social Studies**
Technology By acting out stories that explore the history of medicine, students with various learning styles can learn how early technological advances benefit people today.

★ **Music**
Rhythm and Repetition Students can transfer knowledge of rhythm and repetition to music and use it to create group unity and convey emotional states.

★ **Dance**
Shapes When students use shapes to portray a scene, character, or environment they can also use these shapes as a point of departure for exploring potential movement.

Objectives

 Perception To identify what images can tell us about a character or situation

 Creative Expression To create a movement snapshot through tableau

 History and Culture To use the image of a historical event to create a tableau

 Evaluation To informally evaluate one's own work

Materials

- Copies of **"Movement Snapshots" Warm-Up,** p. 55
- Journals or writing paper

Standards

National Theatre Standard: The student is expected to select movement, music, or visual elements to enhance the mood of a classroom dramatization.

Listening/Speaking Standard: The student interacts with peers in a variety of situations to develop and present familiar ideas (for example, conversations, whole group interactions, discussions).

Social Studies Standard: The student understands the impact of science and technology on life. The student is expected to identify famous inventors and scientists and their contributions.

Lesson 1: Movement Snapshots

Focus
Time: About 10 minutes

"In this lesson we will create instant tableaux to show snapshots of movement." *(See page T7 for more about Tableau.)*

Activate Prior Knowledge

▶ Distribute the **"Movement Snapshots" Warm-Up,** and have students complete it. Encourage them to use their imaginations.

▶ Have students stand and use their character descriptions to move like their characters. Say, "Freeze." Point out thought-provoking poses.

Teach
Time: About 15 minutes

Prepare Divide students into pairs. Designate one-half of the pairs as "Group 1" and the other half as "Group 2."

Lead Tell students that they are going to create "movement snapshots."

▶ Instruct student pairs to choose a favorite book or assign the same book to the entire class. Tell them to choose a scene from that book in which two characters are in conflict. Give them time to plan.

▶ Have Group 1 begin enacting their scenes. When you say "click," they must freeze in place. Allow the other half of the class to examine each "snapshot." Repeat with Group 2.

Informal Assessment Did each pair enact a scene involving conflict and freeze when you said "click"?

History and Culture

Have students go online to find an image of *Louis Pasteur in His Lab* by Albert Edelfelt. Explain that Louis Pasteur's scientific work contributed to the development of the first vaccines. If possible, have students do some brief research on the work of Pasteur. Divide the class into thirds. Have students in each third create tableaux showing what happened directly before, during, and after the scene shown in the painting.

Reflect
Time: About 5 minutes

▶ Discuss details about characters and their relationships. Have students predict what might have happened next.

Apply

Journal: Observing

Have students describe in their journals how a person's movements might be affected by a certain kind of illness or injury and how they could use this observation when acting.

Name _____ Date _____

Movement Snapshots

Look at the picture below. What can you tell about the characters and relationships in this image? Choose one character from the picture and describe this character's feelings, personality, job, and reasons for speech and action on the lines below.

Unit 3 • **Movement** Lesson 1 • Movement Snapshots 55

Objectives

Perception To identify ways movement can communicate the five *W*s

Creative Expression To use dramatic movement to show *who*

History and Culture To learn about Iroquois dance theatre

Evaluation To informally evaluate one's own work

Materials

- Copies of **"Movement and the Five *W*s" Warm-Up,** p. 57
- Journals or writing paper

Unit Links

Visual Arts: Color
Compare and contrast the way actors and dancers can use movement to visually show a character's physical health. Compare and contrast these visual and kinesthetic aspects with the use of color in artwork. How can artists use color to communicate a subject's health? *(A subject who is very healthy might be painted with brightly colored eyes, someone who is pale might look sick, and so on.)* How can musicians create similar feelings of movement?

Standards

National Theatre Standard: The student acts by assuming roles and interacting in improvisations.

Listening/Speaking Standard: The student uses eye contact and gestures that engage the audience.

English Language, Fine Arts and Reading/Writing Standard: The student comprehends selections using a variety of strategies.

Lesson 2: Movement and the Five *W*s

Focus
Time: About 10 minutes

"In this lesson we will use dramatic movement to show *who*." (See page T13 for more about Dramatic Movement.)

Activate Prior Knowledge

▶ Distribute the **"Movement and the Five *W*s" Warm-Up,** and have students read the story.

▶ Discuss ways in which a person's movement could communicate some or all of the five *W*s. *(Bending Willow's paddling movements would indicate she was in a canoe, and so on.)*

Teach
Time: About 15 minutes

Prepare Divide students into two groups.

Lead

▶ Have the members of each group choose a different age, such as baby, child, teenager, adult, or senior. Have each group assign the other group an action, such as walking up a flight of stairs or getting dressed.

▶ Have members of each group take turns performing their action. Encourage them to think about their character's age and emotions, using imagination and personal experience. Is this action easy for the character? Have the other group guess each character's age.

Informal Assessment Did each student use safe, dramatic movement to perform an action and show a certain age?

History and Culture

Explain that many traditional health practices have been found to be scientifically valid. Some of these wise health practices were taught through tales such as "Bending Willow." Have students investigate theatrical traditions of the Iroquois Confederacy that are associated with health and wellness, such as the Jingle Dance, and identify the *who* and *what* represented in these dances. How do these reflect Iroquois culture? If these dances had voices, what would they sound like? Why?

Reflect
Time: About 5 minutes

▶ Have students create a behavior checklist and have each student use it to evaluate his or her own participation.

Apply

Journal: Inferring
Have students write a paragraph describing how an ill child or adult moves when he or she expects to get well.

Movement and the Five Ws

Bending Willow

an Iroquois tale

Once there was an unhappy Iroquois woman named Bending Willow. She was upset because the tribe's cruel chief wanted to marry her. She was also sad because sickness had come to her tribe and killed all of her brothers and sisters.

The chief said an evil spirit was making everyone sick. "My marriage to Bending Willow will scare off the spirit," he said, and the wedding was set.

When Bending Willow heard about this, she went to the forest. She did not believe the chief, and so she decided to run away to the lands across the river.

That night she took her father's canoe and paddled into the wide river. The water moved faster and faster, and she realized that she was being pulled toward the great falls. Thunder filled her ears as she reached the edge. Bending Willow closed her eyes.

Suddenly something lifted her up, and she was carried into a cave behind the waterfall. The water spirit, Cloud-and-Rain, had saved her from the rushing waters.

Bending Willow told Cloud-and-Rain of her people's sickness.

"A wedding will not save your people," Cloud-and-Rain said. "Your chief built your village too close to a swamp. An evil snake lives in the swamp and poisons all your water. Soon your chief will die from the poisoned water."

"How can I save my people?" Bending Willow asked.

"Your tribe must move nearer to these great falls. But before you go home I will teach you about many plant medicines," said Cloud-and-Rain.

When Bending Willow went home, she told everyone what Cloud-and-Rain had said. At first no one believed her, but a few women said they would go with Bending Willow and draw water from a spring far from the swamp. For many months they brought this water to their families. None of their children became sick.

When the evil chief died and a new chief took his place, he decided that Bending Willow was right, and he agreed to move their village. Bending Willow lived the rest of her days near the great falls, caring for sick people with the knowledge that Cloud-and-Rain had given her.

Objectives

 Perception To identify the shapes of a fantasy character

Creative Expression To show shapes in movement using creative movement

 History and Culture To identify and compare the work and influence of two African American dance choreographers

 Evaluation To informally evaluate one's own work

Materials

- Copies of **"Shapes in Movement" Warm-Up,** p. 59
- A rattle or jingle bell
- Journals or writing paper

Standards

National Theatre Standard: The student acts by assuming roles and interacting in improvisations.

Listening/Speaking Standard: The student understands that a variety of messages can be conveyed through mass media. The student interprets messages conveyed through mass media.

English Language, Fine Arts and Reading/Writing Standard: The student is expected to describe mental images that text descriptions evoke.

Lesson 3 Shapes in Movement

Focus
Time: About 10 minutes

"In this lesson we will use creative movement to demonstrate the shapes in the movement of bacteria." *(See page T12 for more about Creative Movement.)*

Activate Prior Knowledge

▶ Explain that in 1898 many people doubted that germs existed.

▶ Distribute the **"Shapes in Movement" Warm-Up,** and read the poem. Explain that *sanguine* means "hopeful." Have students complete their drawings. Discuss movements and shapes of the microbes.

Teach
Time: About 15 minutes

Prepare Have students stand next to their desks.

Lead Say, "Microorganisms, such as bacteria, perform many functions." Tell students that they are going to use their bodies to form the shapes and movements of different types of "bacteria characters."

▶ Assign one of the following bacteria jobs to each student: making people sick, breaking down organic matter, such as leaves, and producing antibiotics to be used as medicine.

▶ Use a rattle or bell to create sounds. Students should match the speed of their "bacteria movement" to the sound's speed. They will stand in one place and rhythmically move their upper bodies.

Informal Assessment Did each student use his or her body to safely move as a bacterium?

 History and Culture

Tell students that many African American performers have changed the face of the performing arts. On the Internet, have some students research Arthur Mitchell, founder of the Dance Theatre of Harlem, while others research Alvin Ailey, founder of the Alvin Ailey American Dance Theatre. Compare how each changed the face of dance. *(Mitchell fused ballet, jazz, and modern dance; Ailey set dances to spirituals.)* Have students compare shapes in each dance style with shapes from their creative movement.

Reflect
Time: About 5 minutes

▶ Have students contrast different shapes created by different types of bacteria. Which shapes do students like best? Have students describe how each moving shape might sound and feel.

Apply

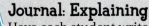 **Journal: Explaining**

Have each student write a journal entry describing the movement of a group of bacteria as it journeys through a human body.

Name _____ Date _____

Shapes in Movement

Read the poem below. How does this poet imagine a microbe would look? Draw your own version of this character in the magnifying glass below.

The Microbe
by Hilaire Belloc

The Microbe is so very small
You cannot make him out at all,
But many sanguine people hope
To see him through a microscope.
His jointed tongue that lies beneath
A hundred curious rows of teeth;
His seven tufted tails with lots
Of lovely pink and purple spots,
On each of which a pattern stands,
Composed of forty separate bands;
His eyebrows of a tender green;
All these have never yet been seen—
But Scientists, who ought to know,
Assure us that they must be so. . . .
Oh! Let us never, never doubt
What nobody is sure about!

Objectives

Perception To identify examples of rhythm and repetition in movement

Creative Expression To show a character's personal rhythm through dramatic movement

History and Culture To identify and apply knowledge of the traditional six areas of the stage

Evaluation To informally evaluate one's own work

Materials

- Copies of **"Rhythm and Repetition" Warm-Up,** p. 61
- Journals or writing paper

Vocabulary

rhythm
repetition

Standards

National Theatre Standard: The student acts by assuming roles and interacting in improvisations.

Listening/Speaking Standard: The student uses eye contact and gestures that engage the audience.

Math Standard: The student uses organizational structures to analyze and describe patterns and relationships.

Lesson 4: Rhythm and Repetition

Focus
Time: About 10 minutes

"In this lesson we will use dramatic movement to show a character's personal rhythm." *(See page T13 for more about Dramatic Movement.)*

Activate Prior Knowledge

▶ Say, "Rhythm in movement involves movements with a certain pattern. Sometimes this pattern includes repetition."

▶ Distribute the **"Rhythm and Repetition" Warm-Up,** and have students complete it. Have volunteers identify other examples of rhythm and repetition in nature.

Teach
Time: About 10 minutes

Prepare Divide students into two groups. Have students clear a space.

Lead Say, "Characters and people in real life have personal rhythms."

▶ Have all students secretly choose an age and personality.

▶ Explain that the area at the front of the room is the side of the highway. Each student should imagine he or she is part of a community group working to clean up this highway. One at a time, members of the first group should begin to pick up trash, allowing their character's age, personality, and emotions to influence their movements. They should not speak.

▶ Repeat the exercise, switching groups.

Informal Assessment Did each student allow a character's personal rhythm to influence his or her movement?

History and Culture

Explain to students that in modern Western theatre, directors and actors use names for areas of the stage to help them communicate about movement. Draw a grid of six boxes and label them from left to right: (top row) Up Right, Up Center, Up Left; (bottom row) Down Right, Down Center, Down Left. Explain that "right" and "left" are an actor's right and left when facing an audience. Stand at the front of the room and call on volunteers to "direct" your movements; have volunteers take your place.

Reflect
Time: About 5 minutes

▶ Have students describe their characters, relationships they formed, and their interactions with the environment.

Apply

Journal: Describing
Have students think about everyday movements, such as walking or playing basketball. Have them write journal entries describing examples of rhythm and repetition in one such movement.

60

Unit 3 • **Movement**

Name _____ Date _____

Rhythm and Repetition

Look at the drawings below. Imagine you were going to move as this running tiger. Describe movements you would use over and over on the lines below.

Objectives

 Perception To identify ways movement can show action and reaction

Creative Expression To demonstrate character reactions using pantomime

 History and Culture To consider movements used to tell stories in Kabuki

 Evaluation To informally evaluate one's own work

Materials

- Copies of **"Action and Reaction" Warm-Up,** p. 63
- Journals or writing paper

Unit Links

Visual Arts: Color
Compare and contrast some ways visual artists, dancers, musicians, and actors in formal and informal theatre can express feelings. Discuss the ways an actor can use movement to show feelings. *(facial expressions, body position)* Explain that color in artwork can show a particular feeling. Have students identify ways in which dancers or musicians can show feelings through their work. *(A dancer can move in a way that seems sad)*

Standards

National Theatre Standard: The student acts by assuming roles and interacting in improvisations.

Listening/Speaking Standard: The student interacts with peers in a variety of situations to develop and present familiar ideas (for example, conversations, whole group interactions, discussions).

Writing Standard: The student writes for a variety of audiences and purposes, and in a variety of forms.

 Lesson 5

Action and Reaction

Focus
Time: About 10 minutes

"In this lesson we will use pantomime to show character reactions." *(See page T3 for more about Pantomime.)*

Activate Prior Knowledge

▶ Say, "Actions produce reactions such as thoughts and feelings. Many times these thoughts and feelings produce movement."

▶ Distribute the **"Action and Reaction" Warm-Up.** Have students complete it, and discuss their answers.

Teach
Time: About 15 minutes

Prepare Divide students into groups of four.

Lead Tell students they will pantomime eating or drinking something, using action and reaction. For example, one student can mime eating an ear of corn and react to it being too hot.

▶ Have groups secretly assign each member something to eat or drink. Remind students to plan their reactions to the food. Is it hot, cold, bitter, rotten, or sweet? Does each character like it? Encourage them to use both their bodies and facial expressions and to interact with each other.

▶ Have groups pantomime eating their meal together. Have other groups guess how they were reacting and why. Remind them to use appropriate audience behavior.

Informal Assessment Did each group member show action and reaction? Did the other groups apply appropriate audience behavior?

 History and Culture

Tell students that one traditional form of Japanese theatre is called *Kabuki*. In Kabuki, actors perform a lively dance and tell a story through their movements. Kabuki plays tell stories about events in history or the everyday life of people long ago. If possible, show images of Kabuki productions on the Internet; have students assume the actors' poses and identify examples of action and reaction in their postures.

Reflect
Time: About 5 minutes

▶ Discuss with students which actions and reactions gave them clues to what each character was eating or drinking.

Apply

Journal: Predicting
Tell students to think of a time they ate something very hot. Have students write a journal entry describing how they reacted to the food and predicting how they could use this experience when acting.

Name _____ Date _____

Action and Reaction

Read each passage below. Describe the action of each character and explain why he or she is acting in this way.

1. The dog limped across the yard as fast as he could. His tail wagged excitedly as he heard his owner calling him for dinner.

_____

_____

_____

_____

2. Zoë held onto her parent's hands tightly as she laughed and danced to the music. She watched the parade of circus elephants walk across the ring.

_____

_____

_____

_____

3. Mohammed's head felt like a boiling pot. He had been up coughing most of the night, so he could barely keep his eyes open. As he rolled over in bed, Mohammed thought about calling his best friend, Adam, later. Adam would tell him what he missed in school.

_____

_____

_____

_____

Unit 3 • **Movement** Lesson 5 • Action and Reaction

Objectives

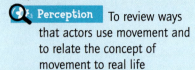

Perception To review ways that actors use movement and to relate the concept of movement to real life

Creative Expression To plan and perform a pantomime

History and Culture To apply research about "The Story of Susan La Flesche Picotte" to the pantomime

Evaluation To thoughtfully and honestly evaluate own participation using the four steps of criticism

Materials

- Copies of **"The Story of Susan La Flesche Picotte,"** pp. 130-133
- A rattle or a jingle bell
- Copies of the **Unit 3 Self-Criticism Questions**, p. 68
- Copies of the **Unit 3 Quick Quiz**, p. 69
- *Artsource®* **Performing Arts Resource Package** (optional)

Lesson 6 — Unit Activity: Dramatized Literary Selection

Focus

Time: About 10 minutes

Review Unit Concepts

"Movement is important in theatre. Actors use movement to physically express a character's mood, age, occupation, or physical state and to show a character's personal rhythm. When actors play nonhuman characters, such as forces in nature, their movements may become less realistic and more dance-like." *"El movimiento es importante en el teatro. Actores usan movimiento para expresar físicamente el humor, la edad, la ocupación o estado físico de un personaje y para mostrar el ritmo personal de un personaje. Cuando los actores hacen el papel de personajes no humanos, como fuerzas de la naturaleza, sus movimientos pueden volver menos realista y más como un baile."*

▶ Review with students the different elements of movement they dramatized in this unit.

▶ Review the unit vocabulary on page 52.

History and Culture

Tell students that "The Story of Susan La Flesche Picotte" is a biography of the first female Native American doctor. The story takes place on the reservation of the Omaha, a Native American tribe, in the late 1800s. Have one group of students research the culture of the Omaha, including details of what their life would have been like at this time; have another group do some simple research about the types of medical practices and beliefs of the late nineteenth century. Allow both groups to use books and the Internet. Have each group report its findings to the class. Discuss ways this research could apply to the **Movement Activity.**

Classroom Management Tips

The following are tips for managing your classroom during the **Rehearsals** and **Activity:**

✔ **Set Ground Rules** Discuss elements of safe movement, such as controlling the speed and force of movement, making sure no one is too close to you, and clearing an appropriate space for an activity. Have students agree to apply it before each movement exercise or activity.

✔ **Encourage Creativity** Tell students not to be afraid to be creative and original in their interpretations of the scenes from the story. The story is the "jumping off" point, but students should add details to each character's actions.

Standards

National Theatre Standard: The student imagines and clearly describes characters, their relationships, and their environments.

64 Unit 3 • Movement

Teach

Time: Two 15-minute rehearsal periods
One 15-minute activity period

First Rehearsal

▶ Distribute copies of **"The Story of Susan La Flesche Picotte"** on pages 130 through 133. Have students follow along as you read the excerpt aloud.

▶ Have students clearly describe the characters, their relationships, the surroundings, and their motivations.

▶ Say, "The action of the storm causes many reactions. What are some of these reactions?" *(Susan cancels school, and so on.)*

▶ Have students clear a space around the edges of the room. Have them begin walking normally in a circle. Tell them you are going to describe the weather's actions, and they should change the way they are walking accordingly.

▶ Describe weather that moves from cloudy and cold to a wild, winter storm, saying things such as, "The wind is beginning to blow harder. Now icy rain is hitting your face." Use a rattle or bell to create sounds that set the pace of the storm's force. Say "freeze" when you want them to stop. Have students discuss the exercise.

Second Rehearsal

▶ Divide students into groups of three. Tell students that they are going to do character work in preparation for a pantomime beginning with Susan leaving the school and ending with her arrival at the Whitefeather's home. *(See page T3 for more about Pantomime.)*

▶ Have students divide the roles of Susan, Jimmy, and Joe. Allow students to adapt roles based on gender, if they wish.

▶ To give students an opportunity to explore their character movement, have them improvise actions each character might use during their time together, such as feeding or changing the baby or feeding and brushing the horse. Tell them to focus on each character's personal rhythm.

Movement Activity

▶ Have students make room in the classroom for the activity. Have them re-form their groups from the **Second Rehearsal.**

▶ Give students a few minutes to plan pantomimes of Susan's journey through the storm. Remind them to use information about Omaha heritage from their research in the **History and Culture** section, as well as the character rhythm they explored in the **Second Rehearsal.**

▶ Allow groups to perform their pantomimes for the class. Remind them to use safe movement and to apply appropriate audience behavior.

▶ Have volunteer groups perform their pantomimes again, switching environment; for example, without preparation, the characters will move through a rainstorm, a tornado, and so on.

Standards

National Theatre Standard: The student acts by assuming roles and interacting in improvisations. The student is expected to imagine and clearly describe characters, their relationships, and their environments.

Unit Links

Visual Arts: Color
Changes in color value can be compared and contrasted with different kinds of movement. Discuss the ways an actor could change the intensity of his or her movements onstage, such as moving slowly or moving fast. Remind students that value is the degree of lightness or darkness of a color. How can an artist use different color values to draw a viewer's attention? *(He or she could use very deep or contrasting values.)*

Theatrical Arts Connection

Television Describe movements in a television program or show an appropriate program with the sound off, and discuss how the movements show characters' thoughts or feelings. What is the role of television in America today? *(entertainment, information)* How do these characters' movements help achieve one of these purposes?

Film Discuss the types of reactive movement used in different movie genres, such as action movies or animated comedies. Do students think they would be able to identify an action movie by watching a short segment of its action? If possible, show clips and have students discuss and identify the genres. Compare and contrast the roles of these types of films in American society.

Standards

National Theatre Standard: The student understands context by recognizing the role of theatre, film, television, and electronic media in daily life.

Reflect

Time: About 10 minutes

Assessment

▶ Have students evaluate their participation by completing the **Unit 3 Self-Criticism Questions** on page 68.

▶ Use the assessment rubric to evaluate the students' participation in the **Unit Activity** and to assess their understanding of movement.

▶ Have students complete the **Unit 3 Quick Quiz** on page 69.

	3 Points	2 Points	1 Point
Perception	Gives full attention to review of unit concepts and vocabulary words. Has mastered the concept of action and physical reaction and can connect it in some way to real life.	Gives partial attention to review of unit concepts and vocabulary words. Is developing an understanding of the concept of action and physical reaction and has trouble connecting it in some way to real life.	Gives little or no attention to review of unit concepts and vocabulary words. Has a poor understanding of the concept of movement and cannot connect it in some way to real life.
Creative Expression	Fully participates in the pantomime using all of the following: body parts, facial expressions, character rhythm.	Fully participates in the pantomime using two of the following: body parts, facial expressions, character rhythm.	Fully participates in the pantomime using one of the following: body parts, facial expressions, character rhythm.
History and Culture	Fully participates in researching either the Omaha culture or nineteenth-century medicine. Clearly utilizes at least two specific details from the class research in the pantomime.	Somewhat participates in researching either the Omaha culture or nineteenth-century medicine. Clearly utilizes at least one specific detail from the class research in the pantomime.	Show poor participation in researching either the Omaha culture or nineteenth-century medicine. Utilizes some aspect of the class research in the pantomime, but does not do it in a clear manner.
Evaluation	Thoughtfully and honestly evaluates own participation using the four steps of art criticism.	Attempts to evaluate own participation, but shows an incomplete understanding of evaluation criteria.	The student makes a poor attempt to evaluate own participation.

Apply

▶ Have students identify movies, television, or live theatre that are based on real-life events in which characters face difficult struggles. Have students identify character movements that illustrate their struggles. Were these events exactly like the events in real life? Why did the screenwriter or playwright change the details?

▶ Have students think of a time in their own lives when they were faced with a difficult situation. Have them discuss how they reacted physically and emotionally to the situation.

View a Performance

Movement in Dance

▶ Have students identify and discuss aspects of appropriate audience behavior. Remind them to listen and watch the performance quietly, and that an audience's job is being respectful of the performers and other audience members.

▶ If you have the **Artsource®** videocassette or DVD, have students view AMAN International Folk Ensemble's "Suite of Appalachian Music and Dance." Have students locate the Appalachian Mountain range on a map. Explain that this music and dance is a mix of different traditional forms from several areas in these mountains.

▶ Discuss the performance with students using the following questions:

Describe What kinds of movements do you see the dancers using? *(foot steps and traveling movements while holding each other's hands or arms, circling, and so on)*

Analyze How do these dancers use rhythm and repetition? *(they repeat many of the steps, they all use the same movements in a line, and so on)* How do the musicians and dancers work together to create a feeling of excitement? *(The music and dance are fast; the dancers call out and clap.)*

Interpret Compare and contrast these theatre artists with ones with which you are familiar. How do dance, music, and theatre show feelings in similar and different ways?

Decide How did it make you feel? Do you think this type of movement would be fun? What kind of play might it belong in?

> "I rely greatly on rhythm. I think that is the one thing I understand: the exploitation of rhythm, change of expression, change of pace in crossing the stage."
>
> —Laurence Olivier (1907–1989), actor/director

LEARN ABOUT CAREERS IN THEATRE

Discuss the differences between actors in musical theatre and actors in non-musical plays. *(the actors dance and sing in musical theatre)* What are the roles of each type of theatre in American society? Explain that a choreographer is a person who plans dance movements in a dance performance or in a musical in which dancing is called for. If possible, show a clip from a recording of an appropriate musical or movie based on a musical, such as *Oklahoma!* or *The Music Man*. Have students identify other issues a choreographer must take into account when planning dance movement for a musical. *(what the audience needs to see, how the dance will help tell the story)* Have student groups research what is necessary to pursue a career in choreography.

Standards

National Theatre Standard: The student understands context by recognizing the role of theatre, film, television, and electronic media in daily life. The student is expected to identify and compare similar characters and situations in stories and dramas from and about various cultures, illustrate with classroom dramatizations, and discuss how theatre reflects life.

Lesson 6 • Unit Activity

Name _____ Date _____

Unit 3 Self-Criticism Questions

Think about how you acted out a scene from "The Story of Susan La Flesche Picotte." Then answer the questions below.

1. **Describe** What types of movement did you use when you acted as your character?

   _____

   _____

   _____

2. **Analyze** How did your character's age, environment, and occupation affect the way you moved?

   _____

   _____

   _____

3. **Interpret** How is your personal rhythm similar to or different than that of your character? Why?

   _____

   _____

   _____

4. **Decide** Would you change anything about the way you showed your character? Why or why not?

   _____

   _____

   _____

Name _____   Date _____

Unit 3   Quick Quiz

Completely fill in the bubble of the best answer for each question below.

1. **Movement can show a character's**
   - A) age.
   - B) feelings.
   - C) environment.
   - D) all of the above.

2. **A character's personal rhythm is not affected by**
   - F) his or her age.
   - G) his or her feelings.
   - H) his or her hair color.
   - J) his or her job.

3. **Repetition in movement is**
   - A) movement that is always funny.
   - B) movement that is done over and over.
   - C) any movement that shows who a character is.
   - D) all of the above.

4. **A tableau is most like**
   - F) a photograph.
   - G) a book.
   - H) a table.
   - J) a movie.

5. **Which of the following is *not* true?**
   - A) Actors use movement to show a character's age.
   - B) Rhythm can mean a pattern of movement.
   - C) Actors sometimes look at people in real life when they are planning character movement.
   - D) An actor never dances onstage.

Score _____ (Top Score 5)

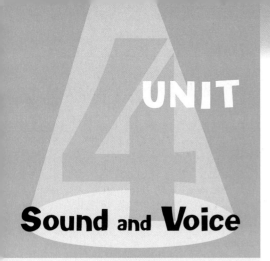

UNIT 4

Sound and Voice

Lesson 1 • Sound and the Five Ws Sound effects can show some of the five *Ws*. *Sound Effects*

Lesson 2 • Sound Shows Setting In theatre, sound effects and music can help establish a play's setting. *Theatre Game*

Lesson 3 • Character Voices Actors use their voices to help portray characters. *Storytelling*

Lesson 4 • Sound Creates Feelings Sound effects can help create mood. *Sound Effects*

Lesson 5 • Tone and Inflection Actors use tone and inflection to communicate a character's ideas and emotions. *Improvisation*

Lesson 6 • Unit Activity: Dramatized Literary Selection This activity will give students the opportunity to use sounds effects, music, and voice in a dramatization.

See pages T3–T20 for more about **Theatre Technique Tips.**

Introduce Unit Concepts

"Sound effects and music can add to the mood of a play, help motivate action, and show setting. Actors' voices convey characters' emotions and ideas." *"Efectos de sonido y música contribuyen al talante de un drama, pueden motivar acción y pueden mostrar como es el ambiente. Las voces de los actores transmiten las emociones e ideas de los personajes."*

Sound and Voice

▶ Ask students what types of sounds they might hear in a play set in an airport. *(jet engines, announcements)*

▶ Have students brainstorm different ways an actor can use his or her voice to communicate how his or her character feels. *(A high, quick voice can show fear, and so on.)* Discuss aspects of safe voice use, such as supporting one's voice with the diaphragm, or stomach muscle, and avoiding strain caused by screaming.

Vocabulary

Discuss the following vocabulary words.

inflection inflexión—changes in a voice's volume and pitch

tone tono—the use of inflection to communicate emotions or ideas

Unit Links

Visual Arts: Form, Texture, and Emphasis

▶ Compare and contrast the use of texture and emphasis to communicate emotions and ideas in theatre, music, and art. Discuss the way sounds are layered in music, and compare and contrast this aural texture with visual texture, such as a painting of rough-looking rocks. Divide students into groups, and have them become sections of an "orchestra." Assign each group a different verbal sound, and act as a "conductor" for this orchestra. Discuss the ways in which their sounds blend together. Explain that sound designers will sometimes choose to emphasize certain sounds.

▶ Show students an image of a sculpture, such as *The Pieta* by Michelangelo. Explain that this is a form because it has three dimensions. Discuss its mood. *(sadness)* Have students create an improvisation to create this same mood, choosing music to emphasize this mood. Have them freeze their improvisation to create a tableau.

Reading Theme: Survival

▶ Discuss extreme survival situations students have seen in movies or read about in books, such as being stranded on a desert island. Have students imagine they were in one such situation. What sounds would they hear? *(waves, birds)*

▶ Identify and discuss a book about survival with which students are familiar, such as *Island of the Blue Dolphins* by Scott O'Dell. How might students use sound effects, music, and voice to help tell the story?

Teacher Background

Background on Sound and Voice

Sound effects, including music, play an important part in theatre. Sounds such as rain pounding on a roof or a wind whistling across a prairie can both help an audience imagine a play's setting and identify with a play's mood. Music may be a part of a play, such as an orchestra playing at a ball, or it may create the background for a scene and set a mood. An actor's use of voice communicates facts about a character, such as age and nationality, but it is the use of vocal tone that communicates a character's emotions and intentions.

Background on Sound Effects

A sound designer is responsible for creating and selecting sound effects and music for a play. Some sound effects help to motivate action onstage; these are known as mechanical sound effects. Sound effects that help to create a play's setting are known as environmental sound effects. Both types of sound help to create a play's illusion of reality.

Research in Theatre Education

"Drama provides opportunities for children to use language for a wider variety of purposes than otherwise typically occurs in classrooms. Drama provides an opportunity to develop expressive language . . ."

—James S. Catterall

on "Nadie Papers No. 1, Drama, Language and Learning. Reports of the Drama and Language Research Project, Speech and Drama Center, Education Department of Tasmania" in *Critical Links*

Differentiated Instruction

Reteach
Give students certain familiar settings, such as the classroom or a school bus, and have them list five sounds that can be heard in that setting based on their observations.

Challenge
Have groups of students choose scenes from different books. Have them create radio dramas for each scene using only sound effects and vocal characterization; ask other students to guess the book.

Special Needs
Students with various cognitive disabilities may benefit from activities in this unit in which they practice listening for and imitating vocal tone and emotional content in people's words.

Theatre's Effects Across the Curriculum

★ **Reading/Writing**
Writing Comprehension Connecting theatre concepts with concepts in real life through journal entries gives students practice in recording, developing, and reflecting ideas.

★ **Math**
Prediction When students work on character voices they use information, such as intentions or emotions, to make predictions about how each character would speak.

★ **Science**
Collecting Information When students use observations of environments to select and create sound effects, they are gathering data through observation.

★ **Social Studies**
Culture Activities based on historical events of various societies allow students to learn about other cultures in an experiential way.

★ **Music**
Research In theatre, students become aware of the importance of clearly communicating setting, mood, and characters, and they may become motivated to research recorded music to support these theatrical components.

★ **Dance**
Non-verbal Communication Speech and dance are two methods of communication; dance is a language that expresses ideas and emotions without requiring words.

Unit 4 • **Sound and Voice**

Objectives

Perception To identify ways sound can show the five Ws

Creative Expression To indicate a setting's five Ws through sound effects

History and Culture To learn about early sound effects in radio broadcasting

Evaluation To informally evaluate one's own work

Materials

- Copies of **"Sound and the Five Ws" Warm-Up,** p. 73
- Tape recorder with a microphone and a blank cassette tape (optional)
- Journals or writing paper

Vocabulary

setting

Standards

National Theatre Standard: The student compares and connects art forms by describing theatre, dramatic media (such as film, television, and electronic media), and other art forms.

Listening/Speaking Standard: The student interacts with peers in a variety of situations to develop and present familiar ideas (for example, conversations, whole-group interactions, discussions).

Writing Standard: The student writes for a variety of audiences and purposes, and in a variety of forms. The student is expected to write to express, discover, record, develop, reflect in ideas, and to problem solve.

Lesson 1: Sound and the Five Ws

Focus
Time: About 10 minutes

"In this lesson we will create sound effects to show some of the five Ws of a setting." *(See page T14 for more about Sound Effects.)*

Activate Prior Knowledge

▶ Distribute the **"Sound and the Five Ws" Warm-Up,** and have students complete it.

▶ Discuss the five Ws related to the illustration and how they could be shown through sound and voice.

Teach
Time: About 15 minutes

Prepare Divide students into groups. If you wish, set up a tape recorder.

Lead Have students use their voices and found objects to create sound effects that illustrate a setting. Each group should choose a setting in which people might survive danger, such as the Franks' secret annex, a rainforest, a ship in stormy seas, and so on.

▶ Have each group list sounds and the five Ws for their setting. Allow time for planning.

▶ Remind students to use their voices safely. Have the rest of the class close their eyes while each group presents its sound effects. If you wish, record their sounds. Allow other students to guess the setting.

Informal Assessment Did each student safely participate in the sound effects creation?

History and Culture

Discuss the role of television in modern life. Tell students that at the time Anne Frank was alive, television had not yet been invented and radio was popular. People could listen to many types of shows, such as detective shows, news broadcasts, or comedy shows. Sound effects helped create a picture in the listener's mind. For example, the sound of a door closing was made by dropping a piano lid or closing a tiny door. Have students discuss the type of show their sound effects in this lesson could enhance.

Reflect
Time: About 5 minutes

▶ If you chose to record, play the tape for students. Discuss with students which sounds gave them clues to each location. Allow them to recreate the sound effects if you wish.

Apply

Journal: Reflecting
Discuss the way sound may remind people of things. Have students, in their journals, reflect on why one particular sound reminds them of something.

Name _____ Date _____

Sound and the Five *W*s

During World War II, many Jewish families in Germany and elsewhere in Europe hid to avoid being sent to concentration camps. When the German Nazis took over Holland, a girl named Anne Frank and her family hid for two years in a secret annex, or hideout, in Mr. Frank's office building. Anne Frank is famous because she kept a diary during this time, and her father published it after her death in a concentration camp.

Look at the illustration below. It shows a view of the secret annex used by Anne and her family. On the lines below, list sounds you might hear if you were in the annex.

_____
_____
_____
_____

Unit 4 • **Sound and Voice** Lesson 1 • Sound and the Five *W*s 73

Objectives

Perception To identify ways sound can show setting

Creative Expression To create sound effects to show setting in a theatre game

History and Culture To learn about the history of radio in California

Evaluation To informally evaluate one's own work

Materials

- Copies of **"Sound Shows Setting" Warm-Up**, p. 75
- Journals or writing paper

Standards

National Theatre Standard: The student is expected to visualize environments and construct design to communicate locale and mood using visual elements (such as space, color, line, shape, and texture) and aural aspects using a variety of sound sources.

Listening/Speaking Standard: The student interacts with peers in a variety of situations to develop and present familiar ideas (for example, conversations, whole group interactions, or discussions).

Reading Standard: The student offers observations, makes connections, reacts, speculates, interprets, and raises questions in response to texts.

74

Lesson 2: Sound Shows Setting

Focus
Time: About 10 minutes

"In this lesson we will play a theatre game in which sound effects show setting." *(See page T5 for more about Theatre Games.)*

Activate Prior Knowledge

▶ Hand out the **"Sound Shows Setting" Warm-Up.** Read the poem aloud, and then have students answer the questions.

▶ Discuss how the nonsense words evoke sounds that illustrate a knight's battle in the "tulgey wood" with the imaginary monster.

Teach
Time: About 15 minutes

Prepare Divide students into groups of four.

Lead Say, "We are going to play a theatre game in which each group will improvise the battle between the knight and the Jabberwock. Two of you in each group will improvise the battle's actions while the other two use their voices to create sound effects." Have the entire class work together on improvising environmental sound effects that could show the setting.

▶ Tell students that although they are going to improvise a battle, they should not actually touch each other. Explain that actors often pretend to fight without hurting each other.

▶ Have all groups play the game simultaneously. After a few minutes, have the actors and sound effects creators switch roles and replay.

Informal Assessment Did each student participate by safely improvising action and creating sound effects?

History and Culture

Explain to students that the first radio broadcasts were in Morse code and used for military communication. That changed in 1909 when Charles "Doc" Herrold, who later called himself the "Father of Radio Broadcasting," decided to broadcast music, talk, and news in San Jose, California, using a homemade transmitting device. His first audience was young students who built their own wireless sets. Compare the role of radio in the 1920s with the role of television in modern America. Explain that they are very similar.

Reflect
Time: About 5 minutes

▶ Discuss with students the way they created sounds. How did they enhance the action and help show setting?

Apply

Journal: Describing
Have students think about their favorite places to visit and describe the types of sounds they would hear there in their journals.

Unit 4 • **Sound and Voice**

Name _____ Date _____

Sound Shows Setting

Warm-Up

Lewis Carroll made up many words in his writings. Even though there are many nonsense words in this poem, think about what pictures they create in your mind as you read the poem. Then answer the questions below.

Jabberwocky

from *Through the Looking Glass*
by Lewis Carroll

Twas brillig, and the slithy toves
Did gyre and gimble in the wabe;
All mimsy were the borogoves,
And the mome raths outgrabe.

"Beware the Jabberwock, my son!
The jaws that bite, the claws that catch!
Beware the Jujub bird, and shun
The frumious Bandersnatch!"

He took his vorpal sword in hand:
Long time the manxome foe
he sought—
So rested he by the Tumtum tree,
And stood awhile in thought.

And as in uffish thought he stood,
The Jabberwock, with eyes of flame,

Came whiffling through the
tulgey wood,
And burbled as it came!

One, two! One, two! And through
and through
The vorpal blade went snicker-snack!
He left it dead, and with its head
He went galumphing back.

"And has thou slain the Jabberwock?
Come to my arms, my beamish boy!
O frabjous day! Calloh! Callay!"
He chortled in his joy.

Twas brillig, and the slithy toves
Did gyre and gimble in the wabe;
All mimsy were the borogoves,
And the mome raths outgrabe.

1. Briefly describe the way you think the setting looks.

_____

2. Describe the sounds a Jabberwock might make.

_____

3. Who is the survivor in the story?

_____

Unit 4 • **Sound and Voice**   Lesson 2 • **Sound Shows Setting**

Objectives

Perception To identify ways voice is used to tell a story

Creative Expression To tell a story using character voices

History and Culture To identify and explore examples of universal characters

Evaluation To informally evaluate one's own work

Materials

- Copies of "Character Voices" Warm-Up, p. 77
- Journals or writing paper

Unit Links

Visual Arts: Texture
Have students compare and contrast the actor's use of voice in theatre with the use of texture in art, dance, and music. Discuss with students the way actors in both formal and informal theatre use vocal texture to communicate character by making their voices sound rough or smooth. Identify types of texture students have seen in sculpture. Discuss the way an orchestra can create aural texture by layering different sounds. Have students describe the way dancers use smooth or staccato movements to create texture in dance.

Standards

National Theatre Standard: The student analyzes and explains personal preferences and constructs meanings from classroom dramatizations and from theatre, film, television, and electronic media productions.

Listening/Speaking Standard: The student listens and speaks both to gain and share knowledge of his/her own culture, the culture of others, and the common elements of cultures. The student is expected to compare oral traditions across regions and cultures.

English Language, Fine Arts and Reading/Writing Standard: The student is expected to read classic and contemporary works.

Lesson 3: Character Voices

Focus
Time: About 10 minutes

"In this lesson we will use character voices to tell a story." *(See page T11 for more about Storytelling.)*

Activate Prior Knowledge

▶ Hand out the **"Character Voices" Warm-Up,** and have students read the selection and follow the directions.

▶ Discuss the importance of voice in storytelling. Have students divide into pairs and briefly paraphrase the stories told while creating the voice of each character.

Teach
Time: About 15 minutes

Prepare Divide students into pairs.

Lead Tell each pair to choose a story to tell based on events that honor one member's heritage or a heritage studied in another curricular area, such as a cultural celebration. They should create characters—one who has participated in this event before and one who has not. Each member in the pair should take a turn describing the event from his or her character's point of view.

▶ Tell students to think about how each character would sound. Have them think about how each character's traits influence his or her vocal speed, volume, and accent. Encourage safe voice use.

▶ Have pairs volunteer to share their stories with the class.

Informal Assessment Did each student develop and assume a character based on heritage and safely participate in the storytelling?

History and Culture

Tell students that storytelling has been an important part of all cultures, especially for cultures that do not have written literature. Discuss the concept of a universal character, or a character type who appears in stories and literature throughout the world, such as the foolish young man or the trickster. If possible, have students identify cultural stories that contain similar characters, and dramatize dialogue from two of these stories. Compare each version of the character.

Reflect
Time: About 5 minutes

▶ Have students describe their characters, their relationships, their environments, and how their stories demonstrated a logical sequence of events.

Apply

Journal: Describing
Have students write a description in their journals of the unique vocal qualities of a person with whom they are close.

Name _____ Date _____

Character Voices

Read the passage, and then follow the directions below.

Storytellers at Sea

from *Captains Courageous* by Rudyard Kipling (Adapted)

An interesting group of men work on the We're Here, *a fishing boat near the coast of Maine. When the days at sea grow stormy, the fishermen Manuel and Salters and the ship's cook tell stories to Harvey, a young boy on the ship.*

Manuel's talk was slow and gentle—about girls in Madeira washing clothes in the dry beds of streams, by moonlight, under waving bananas; tales of odd dances or fights away in the cold Newfoundland ports.

Salters told farm stories, for his mission in life was to prove the value of green fertilizer, and 'specially of clover, against every other kind of fertilizer whatsoever.

The cook naturally did not join in these conversations. As a rule, he spoke only when he had to; but at times a strange gift of speech came on him, and he would speak an hour at a time. He told them of carrying mail in the winter up Cape Breton way, of the dog-train that goes to Coudray, and of the ram-steamer *Arctic*—a boat that breaks the ice in the sea between the mainland and Prince Edward Island. Then he told them stories that his mother had told him, of life far to the southward, where water never froze. That seemed to Harvey a very odd idea for a man who had never seen a palm tree in his life.

Briefly describe the voices of Manuel, Salters, and the cook as you imagine them.

_____

_____

_____

_____

_____

_____

Objectives

 Perception To identify ways sound creates feelings

 Creative Expression To select and use music that creates a certain mood

 History and Culture To research African American history in support of the pantomime

 Evaluation To informally evaluate one's own work

Materials

○ Tape or CD player, a recording of a traditional African American slave song, and recordings of blues music

○ Journals or writing paper

Vocabulary

mood

Unit Links

Visual Arts: Form
Forms in art, body shapes in dance, and music in theatre can create mood. Compare and contrast the way music creates mood with the ways a human sculpture or a dancer's body can evoke mood. Have students create living sculptures with their bodies that evoke the mood from the slave music played during the **Focus** section.

Standards

National Theatre Standard: The student is expected to visualize environments and construct design to communicate locale and mood using visual elements (such as space, color, line, shape, and texture) and aural aspects using a variety of sound sources.

Listening/Speaking Standard: The student is expected to listen to proficient, fluent models of oral reading, including selections from classic and contemporary works.

Social Studies Standard: The student understands the political, economic, and social changes during the last half of the nineteenth century.

Lesson 4 Sound Creates Feelings

Focus
Time: About 10 minutes

"In this lesson we will select music to create a certain mood in a drama." *(See page T14 for more about Sound Effects.)*

Activate Prior Knowledge

▶ Explain to students that the narrator of the introductory quote in what you are about to read was a slave. Read aloud **"Keep Your Eye on the Sun."**

▶ Play the recording of a traditional African American slave song, and discuss how it makes students feel. *(sad, uplifted)* Have students discuss and compare the singing they heard in each recording. Explain that sound effects, including music, create mood, or feelings, for an audience.

Teach
Time: About 25 minutes

Prepare Divide students into groups of four.

Lead Say, "African American slave songs influenced several types of music, including jazz and the blues. I will play two different blues songs; each group will choose one song and decide the mood it creates. What type of story does it make you think of? Create imaginative characters from history and African American heritage, and use safe movement to pantomime a story in which they briefly interact."

▶ Play the blues songs. Allow time for planning, giving suggestions from history with which students are familiar, and have students briefly do the research detailed in the **History and Culture** section below.

▶ Play each group's song while the group pantomimes its story.

Informal Assessment Did each student participate in selecting music and safe movement to create a certain mood?

 History and Culture

During the planning time for their pantomimes, have groups visit safe and accurate Web sites, such as National Geographic's Underground Railroad site www.nationalgeographic.com/railroad/index.html, or search www.yahooligans.com for "civil rights" or "Civil War" and watch the related BrainPOP movies.

Reflect
Time: About 5 minutes

▶ Have students compare and contrast each pantomime's characters, relationships, surroundings, and mood.

Apply

 Journal: Explaining
Have students write journal entries explaining the mood they associate with their favorite songs.

Keep Your Eye on the Sun

from "Music and Slavery" by Wiley Blevins

Mother was let off some days at noon to get ready for spinning that evening. She had to portion out the cotton they was gonna spin and see that each got a fair share. When mother was going round counting the cards each had spun she would sing this song:

Keep your eye on the sun. See how she run. Don't let her catch you with your work undone. I'm a trouble, I'm a trouble. Trouble don't last always.

That made the women all speed up so they could finish before dark catch 'em, 'cause it be mighty hard handlin' that cotton thread by firelight.

—Bob Ellis
slave in Virginia

The life of many slaves in the United States was often full of fear and misery. Long hours were often spent picking cotton in the hot summer sun. At night, the slaves ate what little food their owners had given them and frequently slept on dirt floors. The slaves lived in run-down, overcrowded cabins and owned only the few clothes and possessions their masters had given them. They lived in fear of being beaten if they did not work hard enough or disobeyed their owners. They were not paid, and they were not allowed to leave their homes without special permission.

These terrible living conditions and lack of freedoms made many slaves want to escape. For most, however, there was no real hope of escape. Each day was a struggle to survive. One way the slaves dealt with these hardships was through music. It was a way to express both their sadness and their hope.

The slaves brought with them from Africa a strong tradition of music. Song and dance were an important part of their daily lives. They sang as they worked. They sang to celebrate. They sang when they were sad. They continued this tradition in the new world.

Slaves also brought instruments with them. The drum was the most important instrument used by them in Africa. However, many slave owners believed drums were being used to send secret messages. Therefore, drums were forbidden on most plantations. Instead, slaves kept the strong rhythms of their songs by clapping their hands, stomping their feet, swaying their bodies, and using other instruments such as the banjo. The banjo, developed by the slaves, became a commonly used instrument and is still in use today.

Many of the songs the slaves sang were developed as they worked in the fields. Singing helped take their minds off the difficulties of their work. These songs often changed over time. Many songs required a leader who would sing one line of the song while the others sang the response. These "call and response" chants were unique to slave music. Some songs that survived have become well-known spirituals, or religious songs. These songs, including "Swing Low, Sweet Chariot" and "Go Down, Moses," are based on stories in the Bible in which people were kept as slaves. Slaves were punished, often severely beaten, if they spoke against slavery. Through the spirituals, they could sing about the brutality of slavery without fear of being punished. Many of these songs are still sung today and are a tribute to the rich musical heritage of the slaves.

Objectives

Perception To identify examples of vocal tone and inflection

Creative Expression To perform an improvisation using tone and inflection

History and Culture To compare historical details in a movie and nonfiction writing

Evaluation To informally evaluate one's own work

Materials

- Copies of **"Tone and Inflection" Warm-Up,** p. 81
- Video or DVD player and a recording of *Glory & Honor,* a movie about Matthew Henson
- Journals or writing paper

Vocabulary

tone
inflection

Standard

National Theatre Standard: The student is expected to use variations of locomotor and nonlocomotor movement and vocal pitch, tempo, and tone for different characters.

Listening/Speaking Standard: The student speaks clearly and appropriately to different audiences for different purposes and occasions. The student is expected to use effective rate, volume, pitch, and tone for the audience and setting.

Social Studies Standard: The student understands how people adapt to and modify their environment.

Lesson 5: Tone and Inflection

Focus
Time: About 10 minutes

"In this lesson we will perform an improvisation using tone and inflection." *(See page T4 for more about Improvisation.)*

Activate Prior Knowledge

▶ Distribute the **"Tone and Inflection" Warm-Up,** and have students read it.

▶ Discuss how Matt Henson and the Inuit people must have felt when trying to communicate. *(frustrated, confused)* Say, "A person's tone of voice is the use of inflection to communicate emotional messages." Have volunteers use different tones to say, "I will reach the North Pole."

Teach
Time: About 15 minutes

Prepare Divide students into pairs.

Lead Say, "Think of a physical activity you like and perform often, such as playing one-on-one basketball. How could you explain it to someone who does not know this activity and who does not speak your language, using no props? How could that person ask questions?"

▶ Have each pair divide the roles of teacher and learner. The learner must pretend he or she has never performed this activity. Neither of them is allowed to speak in English; they must use made-up words to communicate. They should limit gestures, as the focus should be on using tone.

▶ Give students one minute to prepare. Then have each pair briefly perform its improvisation. If time allows, have volunteers switch roles and repeat their improvisation.

Informal Assessment Did each student safely participate in the improvisation, using tone or voice to communicate?

History and Culture

If possible, show a clip from the movie *Glory & Honor.* Discuss the way these actors use tone and inflection. Have students compare historical details with details from the **Warm-Up.**

Reflect
Time: About 5 minutes

▶ Have students discuss how tone of voice helped them communicate.

Apply

 Journal: Creative Writing
In their journals, have students write dialogue for a brief, imaginary conversation between two friends. Have students read the dialogue aloud in pairs.

Name _____ Date _____

Tone and Inflection

Planning for the North Pole

In 1909, Matthew Henson became the first African American explorer to reach the North Pole. With Henson were three Inuits from Greenland—Ootah, Egingwah, and Seegloo—who were very good at driving dog sleds. The leader of the group was Commander Robert Peary, a civil engineer and naval officer. Matthew Henson was Peary's field assistant and trail leader.

The North Pole was a very dangerous place, and many people had died trying to make it there. So how did they do it? Peary and Henson had spent many years planning this trip. They had to search the Arctic Ocean for a way to the Pole. They made equipment to use, such as a ship that could crush through ice and special light sleds that could make it across thin ice.

One important reason Robert Peary and Matt Henson were able to make it was because they learned from the Inuit people how to survive in the Arctic. On their first trip to the Arctic, they asked Inuit people to help them.

Matt studied with Inuit teachers. At first he did not speak their language. Communicating was difficult. They had to use hand signs and the tone of their voices to understand each other. The Inuit people were very patient with Matt and worked to teach him.

Slowly Matt learned their language, their ways of eating and hunting, how to drive a sled pulled by huge dogs, and how to build an igloo. The Inuit people knew much about cold weather. They knew what type of animal fur to wear to keep warm. They built stone and ice igloos that were warmer than tents. The Inuit called Matt their brother—they called him "Miy Paluk," which means "dear little Matthew."

Because the Inuit people taught Matt how to survive, he and Peary were able to make safe plans, design equipment, and travel to the North Pole.

Objectives

 **Perception** To review ways sound and voice are used in theatre and to connect sound and voice to real life and written literature

 **Creative Expression** To select and create sound effects and use voice to enhance a dramatization

History and Culture To compare the main character of "On Mars" to a historical figure who was a survivor

Evaluation To thoughtfully and honestly evaluate one's own participation using the four steps of criticism

Materials

- Copies of **"On Mars!"** pp. 134-135
- Tape or CD player and instrumental music to create a mood of excitement, such as a soundtrack for a science fiction movie or television series
- Objects to be used in sound effects creation, such as cellophane, bells, or cups
- Tape recorder with a microphone and four blank tapes
- Copies of the **Unit 4 Self-Criticism Questions,** p. 86
- Copies of the **Unit 4 Quick Quiz,** p. 87
- *Artsource®* Performing Arts Resource Package (optional)

Standards

National Theatre Standard: The student identifies and describes the visual, aural, oral, and kinetic elements of classroom dramatizations and dramatic performances.

Lesson 6 Unit Activity: Dramatized Literary Selection

Focus

Time: About 10 minutes

Review Unit Concepts

"Actors use their voices to create characters. By using tone and inflection, an actor can communicate a character's feelings and emotions. Sound effects, including music, are important in creating mood, showing setting, and motivating action onstage." *"Actores usan sus voces para crear personajes. Usando tono e inflexión, un actor puede comunicar los sentimientos y emociones de un personaje. Los efectos de sonido, incluyendo la música, son importantes para crear el talante, mostrar como es el ambiente y motivar la acción sobre el escenario."*

▶ Review with students the ways they used sound and voice in the dramatic activities in this unit.

▶ Review the unit vocabulary on page 70.

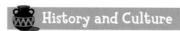 **History and Culture**

Tell students that this lesson's story "On Mars!" is from *A Princess of Mars*. This book is the first book in a series of eleven Martian novels by Edgar Rice Burroughs. It tells the story of John Carter, a Civil War veteran, who is suddenly transported to Mars and has to escape and overcome many dangers. Although John Carter is an imaginary character, many people in real life have survived under similarly confusing and difficult circumstances, such as immigrants who come to America without knowledge of English. Bring in some books or articles about people in history who acted with bravery and helped others through difficult situations. Have students compare and contrast one such person's survival with the survival they dramatized in the **Activity.** Prompt them to use three specific details from the person's experience.

Classroom Management Tips

The following are tips for managing your classroom during the **Rehearsals** and **Activity:**

✔ **Encourage Creativity** As the story takes place on an imaginary version of the planet Mars, students should think about how any imaginary machines and wildlife might sound. Remind them that since they are not creating sound effects for a realistic setting, they can create fantastic sound effects. As an example, have students decide what sound might be created when John Carter walks on this imaginary planet.

✔ **Appropriate Audience Behavior** Tell students to listen quietly and attentively to each group's presentation and show proper respect. Discuss and compare different audience behaviors at different types of performances, both good and bad, and how they affect performers and other audience members.

Teach

Time: One 15-minute rehearsal period
One 20-minute rehearsal period
One 30-minute activity period

First Rehearsal

▶ Distribute copies of **"On Mars!"** on pages 134–135. Have students pantomime the selection in unison as you read the story aloud.

▶ Discuss the story, having students clearly describe the characters, their relationships, and their environment. What problem is John Carter, the main character, faced with? *(He is suddenly on another planet.)* How is life on this imaginary version of Mars different than life on Earth? *(You can jump very high, and so on.)*

▶ Divide the class in half. Have one half improvise rhythmic movement and voice, including wordless sounds for Martian babies, while the other improvises rhythmic movement and voice for adult Martians. Encourage creativity.

Second Rehearsal

▶ Divide students into four groups.

▶ Tell students that they are going to create sound effects and select music to be used in a story dramatization during the upcoming **Activity.** *(See page T14 for more about Sound Effects.)* This dramatization will extend the story. Say, "Think about where the Martians might be taking John. Are they really friendly or did John misunderstand? What music might show an audience the mood of John's true situation? What types of sounds could show this new setting?"

▶ Provide students with objects for creating sound effects, and encourage them to use other objects in the classroom, their voices, and their hands and feet. Give each group five minutes to record their sounds using the tape recorder and a blank cassette tape.

▶ When groups are not recording or planning sounds, have them take turns listening to the music you brought in (with the player set on low volume); each group should select one song to create a mood.

Sound and Voice Activity

▶ Have the class briefly review appropriate audience behavior and create a behavior checklist detailing what is expected from each student while performing and viewing performances.

▶ Have students make room in the classroom for the activity.

▶ Reform groups from the **Second Rehearsal.** Have each group select one person to play the sound effects and music and another person to narrate the story by speaking John Carter's thoughts. Have them divide other roles, reminding them that they are going to extend the story. Tell them to allow the music and sounds to influence their movements.

▶ Allow a few minutes for further planning.

▶ Have each group perform its dramatization for the class, including sound effects. Encourage them to safely use tone to communicate how each character feels.

▶ Have each student apply the behavior checklist to himself or herself.

Standards

National Theatre Standard: The student acts by assuming roles and interacting in improvisations. The student is expected to imagine and clearly describe characters, their relationships, and their environments.

Unit Links

Visual Arts: Emphasis
Discuss with students the sounds they used in the **Sound and Voice Activity.** Which sounds were most important? Review ways that artists may use elements, such as color or texture, for emphasis and to draw a viewer's eye to a certain part of an artwork. Compare and contrast them with the way students used sound in the activity and with the way sound designers could use sound in formal theatre.

Theatrical Arts Connection

Television Show a television commercial that uses sound effects, such as a car commercial. Have students listen to the commercial without seeing it. Then have them describe the sound effects and the actions they enhance. Allow them to watch the commercial, and then discuss the role of the sound effects in the context of the roles of advertising and television in American society.

Electronic Media Have students identify types of sound effects they usually hear in video and computer games. How do they affect their experience of the game? *(make it more exciting or realistic)* Discuss the role of electronic media, such as these games, as entertainment in American society.

Standards

National Theatre Standard: The student understands context by recognizing the role of theatre, film, television, and electronic media in daily life.

Reflect

Time: About 10 minutes

Assessment

▶ Have students evaluate their participation by completing the **Unit 4 Self-Criticism Questions** on page 86.

▶ Use the assessment rubric to evaluate the students' participation in the **Activity** and to assess their understanding of sound and voice.

▶ Have students complete the **Unit 4 Quick Quiz** on page 87.

	3 Points	2 Points	1 Point
Perception	Gives full attention to review of unit concepts and vocabulary words. Masterfully connects these concepts to real life environments and printed dialogue.	Gives partial attention to review of unit concepts and vocabulary words. Adequately connects these concepts to real life environments and printed dialogue.	Gives little attention to review of unit concepts and vocabulary words. Minimally connects these concepts to real life environments and printed dialogue.
Creative Expression	Fully participates in all of the following: creation of sound effects, selection of music, and (in the performance) portrayal of characters, narration, or the running of sound effects.	Participates in two of the following: creation of sound effects, selection of music, and (in the performance) portrayal of characters, narration, or the running of sound effects.	Participates in one of the following: creation of sound effects, selection of music, and (in the performance) portrayal of characters, narration, or the running of sound effects.
History and Culture	Writes a paragraph clearly comparing and contrasting a historical survivor with the survival dramatized in the activity using three details from the person's experience.	Writes a paragraph comparing and contrasting a historical survivor with the survival dramatized in the activity using two details from the person's experience.	Writes a paragraph comparing and contrasting a historical survivor with the survival dramatized in the activity using one detail from the person's experience.
Evaluation	Thoughtfully and honestly evaluates own participation using the four steps of art criticism.	Attempts to evaluate own participation, but shows an incomplete understanding of evaluation criteria.	The student makes a poor attempt to evaluate own participation.

Apply

▶ Have students think about elements that would be used in a play about a difficult day they survived recently. What sound effects would be needed? What type of mood would they want to create through music? Divide students into groups, and have each group select one member's story. Have students use their voices to create music that expresses the mood of that story. Then have them describe how their voices expressed the mood.

▶ Discuss the importance of understanding vocal tone in stories. How can writers indicate a character's tone in a novel or story? *(by using adjectives and punctuation)*

View a Performance

Sound and Voice in Musical Storytelling

▶ Discuss with students aspects of appropriate audience behavior. Have students agree to apply this behavior while listening to the performance.

▶ If you have the *Artsource®* audiocassette or DVD, have students listen to "The Boy Who Wanted to Talk to Whales," a folktale told by the Robert Minden Ensemble. Explain that Robert Minden leads an orchestra of performers who play conventional instruments, found objects, such as cans and saws, and acoustic inventions, such as the Waterphone.

▶ Discuss the performance with students using the following questions:

Describe What types of sounds did you hear? *(clinking, drumming, wavering high sounds, plinking)* What voices did you hear? *(a woman singing, people calling together in a shout, the narrator's voice)*

Analyze How did the sounds and music help show the setting? *(There were sounds like waves and thunder.)* How did they set the mood? *(The woman singing created a sad mood; percussion created a mood of excitement.)*

Interpret Have you ever thought about making music using ordinary objects like cans and springs? Did the Waterphone at the end sound like a whale's song?

Decide Discuss the work of the theatrical artist, Robert Minden. How is it like and unlike the traditional work of a sound designer in theatre? *(Robert Minden makes up his own stories while sound designers usually create sounds for other people's plays, and so on.)* What was your favorite section of the story and why?

LEARN ABOUT CAREERS IN THEATRE

Explain to students that a sound designer's job is to select and create sound effects and music for a theatrical performance. Explain that a sound designer must think about mechanical sound effects, which help motivate action onstage. Have students suggest possible mechanical sound effects that a sound designer might need for a formal theatrical dramatization of "On Mars!" *(the small sound that John hears, which makes him turn around and see the adult Martians)* Explain that a sound designer must also plan environmental sound effects, which help create setting and mood. Discuss possible environmental sound effects for "On Mars!" *(the sound of the animals galloping, a blowing wind)*

"Drama work involves a rich and situated sense of learning how to learn . . . This is part of the joy of drama; it is honest inquiry and we do not know what we will experience or learn when we begin."

—Jeffrey D. Wilhelm, teacher

Standards

National Theatre Standard: The student analyzes and explains personal preferences and constructing meanings from classroom dramatizations and from theatre, film, television, and electronic media productions.

Lesson 6 • Unit Activity

Name _____ Date _____

Unit 4 Self-Criticism Questions

Think about how you participated in creating and choosing sound, music, and character voices for the dramatization of "On Mars!" Then answer the questions below.

1. **Describe** What sound effects did your group create? Describe the music you chose. How did you or others in your group use voice to show character and feelings?

   _____

   _____

2. **Analyze** What did the sound effects and music show about mood and setting? How did your own or others' voices show how characters were feeling?

   _____

   _____

3. **Interpret** Were the sounds like sounds in your everyday life? Why or why not? If you acted, how is your own voice like that of your character?

   _____

   _____

4. **Decide** Would you change anything about how you used sound, music, or voice? What would you change and why?

   _____

   _____

Name _____ Date _____

Unit 4 Quick Quiz

Completely fill in the bubble of the best answer for each question below.

1. Actors use their voices to
- (A) show who a character is.
- (B) show feelings.
- (C) tell a story.
- (D) all of the above

2. Which of the following is *not* true?
- (F) Sound effects can show setting.
- (G) Music can make a play seem scary.
- (H) Sound effects cannot create mood.
- (J) Music can be used during a movie's climax.

3. Tone is
- (A) a special kind of background music.
- (B) another name for a sound effect.
- (C) a character's silent thoughts and secret feelings.
- (D) the use of a voice's inflection to communicate feelings.

4. Inflection is
- (F) not used by people in real life.
- (G) a voice's pitch and volume.
- (H) the place where a story happens.
- (J) another name for shouting.

5. Sound and voice
- (A) do not help show the five *W*s.
- (B) are always recorded.
- (C) help tell the story of a play.
- (D) none of the above

Score _____ (Top Score 5)

UNIT 5
Visual Elements

Lesson 1 • **Setting** Visual elements help show a play's setting. *Setting*

Lesson 2 • **Props** Actors use personal props in plays. *Props*

Lesson 3 • **Visual Elements and the Five Ws** Props and scenery help show *when* and *where* a play happens; costumes help show *who* the characters are. *Setting*

Lesson 4 • **Costumes** A character's clothing can communicate many things about the character. *Costumes*

Lesson 5 • **Masks and Makeup** Other costume elements, such as masks and makeup, help turn an actor into his or her character. *Masks and Makeup*

Lesson 6 • **Unit Activity: Improvisation** This activity will give students the opportunity to use visual elements in an improvisation based on literature.

See pages T3–T20 for more about **Theatre Technique Tips.**

Introduce Unit Concepts

"Props, scenery, and costume items, including clothing, masks, and makeup, are all visual elements of theatre. They create visual interest and help to communicate a play's setting, mood, and characters." "Los props, la escenografía y los elementos del vestuario, incluyendo ropa, máscaras y maquillaje, son todos elementos visuales de teatro."

Visual Elements

▶ Remind students that setting is the time and place in which a story happens. Discuss items that communicate setting onstage. *(Kitchen appliances would show a scene was set in a kitchen, and so on.)*

▶ Discuss the ways objects onstage and the clothing, hats, and makeup worn by actors can help show some of the five *W*s of a play. *(A corseted gown would make an actor seem to be from the 1800s, and so on.)*

Vocabulary

Discuss the following vocabulary words.

floor properties propiedades del piso—usually called "floor props"; objects found onstage, such as a lamp or furniture

personal properties propiedades personales— usually called "personal props"; objects used by an actor

scenery la escenografía—painted boards, screens, or three-dimensional objects that form a stage's background

Unit Links

Visual Arts: Space, Proportion, and Distortion

▶ Tell students that proportion concerns the size relationships of one part of an artwork to another; distortion is a change from expected proportions. Discuss how a scenery designer could use distortion. *(Walls could be much bigger than normal to make actors look like children, and so on.)* How can dancers and musicians use distortion? *(unusual dance movements, disharmonious musical chords)*

▶ Show students the image of a painting, such as *Sir William Pepperrell and His Family* by John Singleton Copley. Discuss the use of space. Discuss what the clothing communicates. Have students move as the characters.

Reading Theme: Communication

▶ Discuss the ways students can communicate with others. *(speaking, writing, drawing, gesturing)*

▶ Have students share examples of books or movies in which characters overcome difficulties in order to communicate. *(The Miracle Worker, and so on.)*

Teacher Background

Background on Visual Elements
Visual elements refer to anything that can be seen onstage, such as props, scenery, costumes, and makeup. The use of visual elements varies from production to production—some play productions contain elaborate and realistic scenery and props, while others may have actors in realistic costumes on a bare stage. Visual elements can help prepare an audience for a play's theme and mood.

Background on Set Designing
Set designers can create the scenery for many types of theatrical productions, including operas, musicals, films, and music videos. Although set designers can design scenery and props that are very realistic, some designers choose to design abstract or symbolic sets that strike a mood rather than recreate reality. Set designers may create walls or backgrounds onstage using flats, or frames covered with painted canvas, muslin, or wood. They also use three-dimensional scenery, such as stair units or trees.

Research in Theatre Education
"The arts serve to broaden access to meaning by offering ways of thinking and ways of representation consistent with the spectrum of intelligences scattered unevenly across our population . . ."

—James S. Catterall, Richard Chapleau, and John Iwanaga

"Involvement in the Arts and Human Development: General Involvement and Intensive Involvement in Music and Theatre Arts."

Differentiated Instruction

Reteach
Have students choose a scene from a movie version of *Beauty and the Beast* and describe the visual elements, such as scenery, props, makeup, and costumes.

Challenge
Have students create or select a plot that involves a mystery and imagine they were creating a play version of that plot. Have them design or create a shoebox diorama version of a set for this play version.

Special Needs
Some students with disabilities may excel in set, costume, or puppet design. Be sensitive to their abilities and preferences, giving them opportunities to perfect their newfound talents.

Theatre's Effects Across the Curriculum

★ **Reading/Writing**
Writing Comprehension Expressing ideas in their journals gives students practice in recording, developing, and reflecting upon their ideas.

★ **Math**
Geometry Creating visual pictures for dramatizations requires students to identify and work with shapes, lines, and patterns.

★ **Science**
Observation When students select or create scenery and props, they use observations from their own or others' environments.

★ **Social Studies**
Technology Learning about developments in communication gives students an opportunity to think about advances in technology and how they have affected theatre.

★ **Music**
Space and Silence As students learn restraint in their use of scenery, they will better understand the need for rests and silent sections in music that emphasize the prominent musical theme.

★ **Dance**
Props and Sets Students can incorporate various props, such as long hair, trash cans, or a broom, into a dance.

Objectives

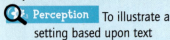 **Perception** To illustrate a setting based upon text

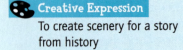 **Creative Expression** To create scenery for a story from history

🏛 **History and Culture** To learn about European attitudes toward scenery from the late 1600s to the 1800s

💬 **Evaluation** To informally evaluate one's own work

Materials

- Copies of "Setting" Warm-Up, p. 91
- Two large sheets of paper (ideally 5' x 5'); nontoxic markers
- Journals or writing paper

Vocabulary

setting
scenery

Unit Links

Visual Arts: Space
Explain that artists sometimes use space in paintings to communicate relationships. Discuss the way a scenic designer could arrange props, such as chairs, onstage to show character relationships. *(Characters that do not get along may sit far apart.)* How could the placement of dancers communicate similar ideas?

Standards

National Theatre Standard: The student is expected to visualize environments and construct design to communicate locale and mood using visual elements (such as space, color, line, shape, texture).

Listening/Speaking Standard: The student uses eye contact and gestures that engage the audience.

Visual Arts Standard: The student develops and organizes ideas from the environment.

Lesson 1 Setting

Focus
Time: About 10 minutes

"In this lesson we will create a setting." *(See page T17 for more about Settings.)*

Activate Prior Knowledge

▶ Remind students that setting is the time and place in which a story happens; scenery is the objects that form a background onstage.

▶ Distribute the **"Setting" Warm-Up,** and have students complete it. Have students explain their designs using information from the text.

Teach
Time: About 20 minutes

Prepare Divide students into two groups. Have them create a safe work environment. Give each group a sheet of paper and markers.

Lead Say, "A play about Koko could show a theme or idea related to communication. Think of another story that could be used in a play about communication, such as a story about Helen Keller or a story quilt. Identify the characters, their actions, and where the play takes place."

▶ Give each group five minutes to decide on an appropriate story from history. Challenge the groups to create their backdrops in fifteen minutes. Tell them to focus on outlining any objects, such as windows.

▶ Hang each backdrop at the front of the room and have each group improvise a scene from their story in front of its backdrop.

Informal Assessment Did each student safely participate in selecting a story and creating scenery?

🏺 History and Culture

Tell students that from the late 1600s to the 1800s, scenic backdrops in England, Italy, and France were very general because people believed specific times and places were not important in drama. Most theatres had a set stock of scenery, including scenery showing city walls, streets, and gardens. Compare this with students' observations of modern uses of setting in plays and movies and discuss how each reflects culture.

Reflect
Time: About 5 minutes

▶ Discuss how each group's scenery defines the characters, their actions, their environment, and the theme or idea of communication.

Apply

📓 **Journal: Designing**
In their journals, have students design fantasy scenery for an imaginary story.

Unit 5 • Visual Elements

Name _____ Date _____

Setting

Read the passage about Koko. Design scenery you would use for a play about Dr. Patterson's work with Koko.

Warm-Up

In 1972, a young woman named Dr. "Penny" Patterson began teaching Koko, a female gorilla, American Sign Language. Penny wanted to see if she could communicate with Koko.

Koko turned out to be much smarter than anyone thought. Koko knows over 1,000 signs and can understand 2,000 spoken words. She has used signs to communicate her thoughts and feelings.

Koko lives in a special trailer at The Gorilla Foundation in Woodside, California. Woodside is in the Santa Cruz Mountains, and Koko has two outdoor play areas. She has her own chairs, tables, and toys. She uses blankets to build a nest each night.

Koko is very happy learning, playing, and talking with Penny. Penny's work with Koko has helped prove that gorillas are much smarter than people ever imagined!

Objectives

 **Perception** To identify props for a dramatized story

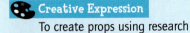 **Creative Expression** To create props using research

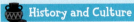 **History and Culture** To learn how props showing communication changed based on technical advances

 **Evaluation** To informally evaluate one's own work

Materials

- Copies of **"Props" Warm-Up,** p. 93
- Materials for prop creation, including items such as string, bendable wire, chenille stems, sheets of cardboard, and wooden spools
- Safety scissors
- Journals or writing paper

Vocabulary

floor prop
personal prop

Standards

National Theatre Standard: The student is expected to collaborate to establish playing spaces for classroom dramatizations and to select and safely organize available materials that suggest scenery, properties, lighting, sound, costumes, and makeup.

Listening/Speaking Standard: The student prepares for and gives presentations for specific occasions, audiences, and purposes (including, but not limited to, group discussions, informational or dramatic presentations).

Social Studies Standard: The student understands the impact of science and technology on life. The student is expected to identify famous inventors and scientists.

Lesson 2: Props

Focus
Time: About 10 minutes

"In this lesson we will create props." *(See page T20 for more about Props.)*

Activate Prior Knowledge

▶ Say, "In theatre, floor props are objects found on stage. Personal props are objects used by actors."

▶ Hand out the **"Props" Warm-Up.** Read the story aloud as students follow along. Discuss the types of props students might use when dramatizing this story.

Teach
Time: About 20 minutes

Prepare Divide students into groups of three.

Lead Tell students that they are going to create a prop that looks like the device Bell used (shown in the diagram below the story).

▶ Provide groups with materials for prop creation. Tell them to do their best to create at least one part of the device, such as the part labeled C. Remind them to work together safely.

▶ Have as many groups as possible dramatize the excerpt using their prop. One student in each group should create the sound effects while the other two act as Bell and Watson.

Informal Assessment Did each group safely create a prop?

History and Culture

Explain that when people in theatre create props for plays set in different places and times, they often have to do research to find out what the props would have looked like. Have students imagine they are going to create or find two telephone props—one for a play set in 1920 and another for a play set in 1950. Have students do an image search on the Internet to find images on which they could base their props, identifying the technical advances that would be illustrated by their props.

Reflect
Time: About 5 minutes

▶ Have students describe the challenges they faced when making their prop. Discuss reasons for safe prop use. *(The prop might be breakable; the prop could hurt an actor.)*

Apply

Journal: Imagining
Have students describe in their journals how different their lives would be without objects such as telephones or computers.

Unit 5 • **Visual Elements**

Props

The Telephone is Born

from *The History of the Telephone* by Herbert Newton Casson (Adapted)

In the year 1875, a tall young professor of speech was busy in a noisy machine-shop that stood in one of the narrow streets of Boston. It was a very hot afternoon in June, but the young professor had forgotten the heat and the grime of the workshop. He was making a machine—a sort of harmonica with a clock-spring reed, a magnet, and a wire. It looked like a silly toy. The young professor had been working on it for three years until, on this hot afternoon in June, 1875, he heard a sound—a faint TWANG—come from the machine.

For an instant he was stunned. He had been expecting just such a sound for several months, but it came so suddenly. His eyes blazed with delight, and he sprang to the next room in which stood a young mechanic who was assisting him.

"Snap that reed again, Watson," cried the young professor. There was one of the odd-looking machines in each room, and the two were connected by an electric wire. Watson had snapped the reed on one of the machines and the professor had heard from the other machine exactly the same sound. It was no more than the gentle TWANG of a clock-spring, but it was the first time in the history of the world that a complete sound had been carried along a wire, created again perfectly at the other end, and heard by an expert in the science of sound.

That twang of the clock-spring was the first tiny cry of the newborn telephone. The professor-inventor was Alexander Graham Bell. Here all the waves of a sound had been carried along a wire and changed back to sound at the farther end. It was crazy. It was incredible. But it was true.

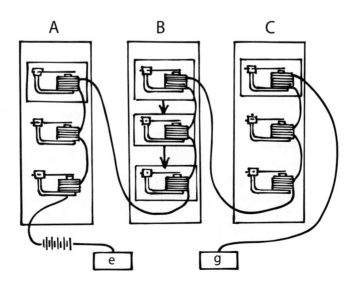

Objectives

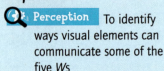

Perception To identify ways visual elements can communicate some of the five Ws

Creative Expression To create a setting and tableau to show *where*

History and Culture To learn about nonrealistic set design

Evaluation To informally evaluate one's own work

Materials

○ Poster board and nontoxic markers (optional)

○ Journals or writing paper

Standards

National Theatre Standard: The student is expected to identify and compare similar characters and situations in stories and dramas from and about various cultures, illustrate with classroom dramatizations, and discuss how theatre reflects life.

Listening/Speaking Standard: The student is expected to listen to proficient, fluent models of oral reading, including selections from classic and contemporary works.

Language Arts Standard: The student is expected to develop vocabulary by listening to selections read aloud.

94

Lesson 3: Visual Elements and the Five Ws

Focus
Time: About 10 minutes

"In this lesson we will create a setting for a tableau that shows *where*." *(See page T17 for more about Settings.)*

Activate Prior Knowledge

▶ Read **"The Burning of the Rice Fields"** aloud.

▶ Have students identify the five *W*s and how props and scenery could illustrate them.

Teach
Time: About 15 minutes

Prepare Divide the class in half.

Lead Have the class choose a scene to dramatize from "The Burning of the Rice Fields." Explain that half of the class will select props while the other half will create scenery.

▶ Give the scenery group poster board and markers or allow them to draw a background on the board. Encourage the prop group to add props not specifically mentioned in the story and to use items imaginatively; for example, a pencil could be the "burning brand."

▶ Have each group act out the scene in front of the scenery while using the props safely. When you say "freeze," they should create a tableau. Have students use each tableau to describe the five *W*s, including characters, their relationships, and their environment.

Informal Assessment Did each student participate in selecting props or creating scenery? Did each student safely use the props and scenery when creating the tableau?

History and Culture

Tell students that sometimes set designers create sets that do not focus on the five *W*s, but instead highlight abstract aspects such as theme. As an example, explain that in medieval Japan, stories were retold through scroll paintings. Have students view the image of a scroll painting on the Internet or in a book. Discuss how a set designer could use this image to create scenery for a dramatization of this lesson's story.

Reflect
Time: About 5 minutes

▶ Have students compare and contrast the two tableaux. Discuss and analyze behavior as audience members.

Apply

Journal: Identifying
Have students make a list of props they would use when dramatizing a particular real-life story in which communication saved someone's life.

Unit 5 • **Visual Elements**

The Burning of the Rice Fields

a Japanese story retold in *How to Tell Children Stories* by Sara Cone Bryant

Once there was a good old man who lived up on a mountain, far away in Japan. All round his little house the mountain was flat, and the ground was rich; and there were the rice fields of all the people who lived in the village at the mountain's foot. Mornings and evenings, the old man and his little grandson, who lived with him, used to watch the blue sea which lay all round the land, so close that there was no room for fields below, only for houses. The little boy loved the rice fields dearly for he knew that all the good food for all the people came from them; and he often helped his grandfather to watch over them.

One day, the grandfather was standing alone before his house, looking far down at the people, and out at the sea, when, suddenly, he saw something very strange far off where the sea and sky meet. Something like a great cloud was rising there. The old man turned and ran to the house. "Yone, Yone!" he cried, "bring a brand from the hearth!"

The little grandson could not imagine what his grandfather wanted with fire, but he always obeyed, so he ran quickly and brought the brand. The old man already had one, and was running for the rice fields. Yone ran after. But what was his horror to see his grandfather thrust his burning brand into the ripe dry rice, where it stood.

"Oh, Grandfather, Grandfather!" screamed the little boy, "what are you doing?"

"Quick, set fire! Thrust your brand in!" said the grandfather.

Yone thought his dear grandfather had lost his mind, and he began to sob; but he thrust his torch in, and the sharp flame ran up the dry stalks, red and yellow. In an instant, the field was ablaze, and thick black smoke began to pour up on the mountain side. It rose like a cloud, black and fierce, and in no time the people below saw that their precious rice fields were on fire. Ah, how they ran! Men, women, and children climbed the mountain, running as fast as they could to save the rice.

And when they came to the mountain top, and saw the beautiful rice-crop all in flames, beyond help, they cried bitterly, "Who has done this thing? How did it happen?"

"I set fire," said the old man, very solemnly; and the little grandson sobbed, "Grandfather set fire."

But when they came fiercely round the old man, with "Why? Why?" he only turned and pointed to the sea. "Look!" he said.

They all turned and looked. And there, where the blue sea had lain, so calm, a mighty wall of water, reaching from earth to sky, was rolling in. No one could scream, so terrible was the sight. The wall of water rolled in on the land, passed quite over the place where the village had been, and broke, with an awful sound, on the mountain side. One wave more, and still one more, came; and then all was water, as far as they could look, below; the village where they had been was under the sea.

But the people were all safe. And when they saw what the old man had done, they honored him above all men for the quick wit which had saved them all from the tidal wave.

Objectives

 **Perception** To solve a costume design problem

 **Creative Expression** To create costume pieces for fairy tale characters

 **History and Culture** To explore how costumes can help actors synthesize real life in theatre

 **Evaluation** To informally evaluate one's own work

Materials

- Copies of **"Costumes" Warm-Up,** p. 97
- Colored pencils or nontoxic markers
- Ribbons and a hole punch
- Poster board and safety scissors
- Stapler (for teacher use)
- Journals or writing paper

Standards

National Theatre Standard: The student is expected to collaborate to establish playing spaces for classroom dramatizations and to select and safely organize available materials that suggest scenery, properties, lighting, sound, costumes, and makeup.

Listening/Speaking Standard: The student interacts with peers in a variety of situations to develop and present familiar ideas (for example, conversations, whole group interactions, discussions).

Fine Arts Standard: The student is expected to integrate a variety of ideas about self, life events, family, and community in original artwork.

 ### Lesson 4

Costumes

Focus
Time: About 10 minutes

"In this lesson we will design costumes." *(See page T18 for more about Costumes.)*

Activate Prior Knowledge
▶ Hand out the **"Costumes" Warm-Up,** and have students use colored pencils or markers to complete it. Discuss student designs and the types of problems a costume designer has to solve.

Teach
Time: About 15 minutes

Prepare Divide students into pairs. Give each pair two sheets of poster board.

Lead Tell students that each pair will create costume pieces for two characters from a fairy tale using the poster board.

▶ Encourage students to think about different costume items such as hats, bracelets, shoes, and so on. Move from pair to pair with a stapler and staple parts of student costumes. Have students punch holes and use the ribbon to tie pieces on as needed. Remind them to use the costume pieces safely and think about how they can help define character, action, and the main idea, or theme.

▶ Have each pair simultaneously put on their costume pieces and improvise a conversation that takes place between their characters.

Informal Assessment Did each pair work together to create costume pieces and then improvise a conversation?

History and Culture

Discuss the similarities and differences between live theatre and real life. Have students think about the clothing they are wearing and, using the question "What if?" imagine characters with a different cultural heritage who might wear the same clothing. Have students assume the roles of these characters and interact with each other, using their imagined character traits to predict the way they will move and speak.

Reflect
Time: About 5 minutes

▶ Discuss how each costume piece helped define character, action and movement, and environment. How could they show a central idea?

Apply

Journal: Designing
Students should write in their journals possible career choices and design costumes based on each career.

Name _____ Date _____

Costumes

Imagine the actor below was playing the character of the Little Mermaid in a play. How could a costume communicate who the character is while allowing the actor to walk onstage? Design a costume that solves this problem.

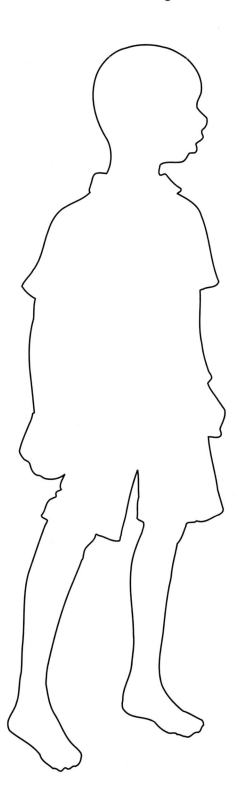

Objectives

Perception To identify the reasons actors wear makeup or masks

Creative Expression To design masks based on scary characters

History and Culture To learn about Puerto Rican *vejigante* masks

Evaluation To informally evaluate one's own work

Materials

- Copies of **"Masks and Makeup" Warm-Up,** p. 99
- Colored pencils, nontoxic markers, and safety scissors
- Sequins, glitter, feathers, and nontoxic glue (optional)
- Journals or writing paper

Unit Links

Visual Arts: Proportion
Compare and contrast the use of proportion to communicate ideas in visual art, formal and informal theatre, and dance. Discuss the ways makeup or mask designers must take into account human facial proportions. Discuss the use of human proportion in artwork and dance.

Standard

National Theatre Standard: The student communicates information to peers about people, events, time, and place related to classroom dramatizations.

Listening/Speaking Standard: The student connects his or her own experiences, information, insights, and ideas with those of others through speaking and listening.

Fine Arts Standard: The student expresses ideas through original artwork, using a variety of media with appropriate skill.

Lesson 5: Masks and Makeup

Focus
Time: About 10 minutes

"In this lesson we will design masks for scary characters." *(See page T19 for more about Makeup and Masks.)*

Activate Prior Knowledge

▶ Say, "Actors can use makeup, wigs, pretend facial hair, false noses or chins, and other techniques to create characters." Discuss with students any times they have worn makeup when going to a costume party.

Teach
Time: About 15 minutes

Prepare Hand out the **"Masks and Makeup" Warm-Up.** Make sure all students have access to markers, colored pencils, safety scissors, sequins, feathers, and glue.

Lead As a class, choose a story or book in which there are scary characters. (Alternatively, reread "Adventure in the Wild Wood" on page 124.)

▶ Have each student design a mask for a character from this story on his or her **Warm-Up.** Tell students that they may make the mask bigger than the outline. Encourage creativity. Have them cut out their masks, including the holes for their eyes and glue on objects such as sequins or feathers. Allow time for drying.

▶ Have students hold their masks in front of their faces and make sure they can safely see through the eye holes. As a class dramatize a scene from the story using rhythmic, expressive movement.

Informal Assessment Did each student create a mask?

 History and Culture

Masks have been an important part of drama in many cultures. Have students locate images of Puerto Rican *vejigante* (pronounced ve-hee-GAN-teh) masks—scary festival masks made of papier-maché or coconut husks. The coconut-shell designs used by people from Loíza are influenced by the town's African and Hispanic heritage. Have students incorporate one aspect of these designs in their masks.

Reflect
Time: About 5 minutes

▶ Have students compare and contrast their masks.

Apply

Journal: Describing
In their journals, have each student describe a mask he or she wore once and how it affected the way he or she felt and moved.

Unit 5 • **Visual Elements**

Name _____ Date _____

Masks and Makeup

Create a mask for a scary character.

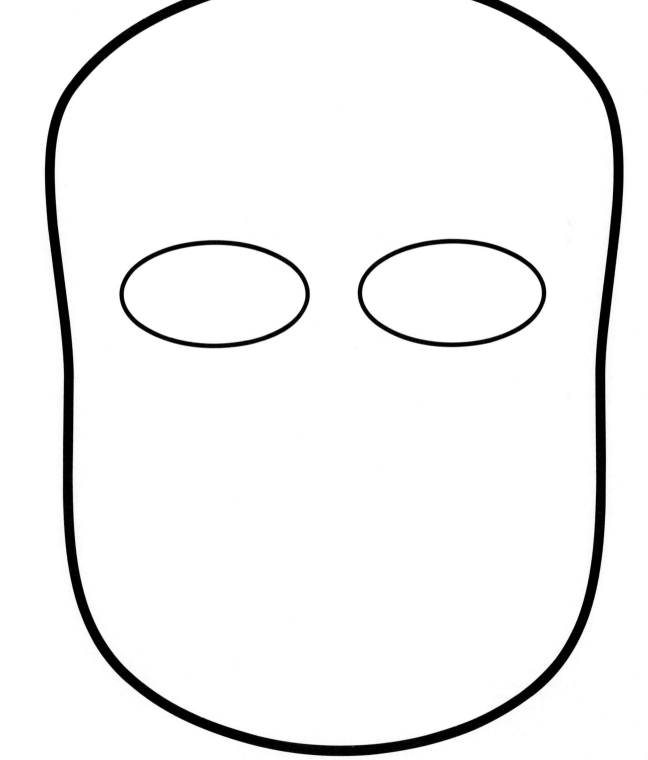

Unit 5 • **Visual Elements**　　　　Lesson 5 • Masks and Makeup

Objectives

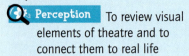 **Perception** To review visual elements of theatre and to connect them to real life

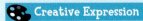 **Creative Expression** To create an improvisation based on a literary selection using visual elements

 **History and Culture** To compare "Animal Language" to ways real animals communicate

 **Evaluation** To thoughtfully and honestly evaluate own participation using the four steps of criticism

Materials

- Copies of **"Animal Language,"** pp. 136–138
- Large paper grocery bags, safety scissors, and markers
- Face paint, makeup remover, cotton balls, and as many mirrors as possible
- A large sheet of paper for scenery creation
- Video or DVD player and a recording of a musical, such as *Cats: The Musical*
- A video game based on a film and a recording of the film on which the game is based (optional)
- Copies of the **Unit 5 Self-Criticism Questions,** p. 104
- Copies of the **Unit 5 Quick Quiz,** p. 105
- *Artsource®* Performing Arts Resource Package (optional)

Standards

National Theatre Standard: The student is expected to collaborate to establish playing spaces for classroom dramatizations and to select and safely organize available materials that suggest scenery, properties, lighting, sound, costumes, and makeup.

Lesson 6 Unit Activity: Improvisation

Focus

Time: About 10 minutes

Review Unit Concepts

"Props, scenery, costumes, and makeup are all visual elements of drama. They help the audience understand a play's setting, mood, and characters." **"Los props, la escenografía y maquillaje son todos elementos visuales de drama. Ayudan al público a entender el marco escénico, el talante y los personajes de un drama."**

► Review with students the different visual elements they utilized in this unit.

► Review the unit vocabulary on page 88.

History and Culture

"Animal Language" is a fictional story about a doctor who can communicate with animals. Have students think of ways animals communicate with them. Prompt them to think of their own or a friend's pet. Ask, "How does a pet tell someone it is hungry, thirsty, happy, or sad?" Ask students to write a paragraph describing the type of communication used by a particular animal, comparing it with three ways animals communicate in "Animal Language." Have them explain how they can use these real-life observations when creating visual elements for the dramatization.

Classroom Management Tips

The following are tips for managing your classroom during the **Rehearsals** and **Activity.**

✔ **Encourage Safety** Remind students to use their props, costumes, and other visual elements safely. Provide students with smocks or old T-shirts when applying makeup or working on the costumes and scenery.

✔ **Encourage Creativity** Remind student groups that even though each member of a group is playing the same type of animal, their costumes and makeup designs may all look very different.

✔ **Take the First Risk** Create your own costume to use when playing Doctor Doolittle. Participate fully in the improvisation, changing the way you speak and move when you act as the doctor.

Teach

Time: Two 15-minute rehearsal periods
One 15-minute activity period

First Rehearsal

▶ Distribute copies of **"Animal Language"** on pages 136–138. Have students follow along as you read the story aloud.

▶ Discuss the story. Have students clearly describe the characters, their relationships, their environment, and the story's sequence of events.

▶ Divide students into pairs. Tell them to think about the types of props the doctor would have used when he examined the plow-horse and to select objects from the classroom that could be used imaginatively as these props.

▶ Have each pair use these props safely and dramatize the doctor's conversation with the plow-horse first in English, and then speaking with neighing sounds (as their conversation would have sounded to another person). Remind them to move as a doctor or horse, using tone and facial expressions to communicate meaning.

▶ Discuss how the props helped define a central idea of communication.

Second Rehearsal

▶ Divide students into groups of four. Tell each group to choose an animal that Doctor Doolittle might have treated.

▶ Have each group work together to design simple makeup (using face paint) and costumes (using large paper bags) for their animal. Provide each student with a paper bag, safety scissors, markers, and any other decoration objects and have them create their costumes, cutting holes in the sides of the bag for their arms. *(See page T19 for more about Makeup and Masks and page T18 for more about Costumes.)*

Visual Elements Activity

▶ Have students clear a space for the improvisation, and have them re-form their groups from the **Second Rehearsal.**

▶ As a class, discuss how the doctor's office would have looked. Would he have any special decorations that would appeal to his animal clients?

▶ Lay out a large sheet of paper, and have volunteers incorporate the class's ideas and draw scenery to represent the back wall of the doctor's office. While these volunteers create the scenery, have other students put on smocks or old clothing, apply their makeup, and put on their costumes. Provide as many mirrors as possible.

▶ Hang the scenery at the back of the cleared space. Have students work together to arrange props in the doctor's office, such as chairs or a desk, while the volunteers who created the scenery put on their makeup and costumes.

▶ Explain that you will act as the doctor in this improvisation; each animal group should come in, explain how they are sick, and you will prescribe their treatment. Remind students to speak and move as animals.

Standards

National Theatre Standard: The student is expected to imagine and clearly describe characters, their relationships, and their environments.

Lesson 6 • Unit Activity

Unit Links

Visual Arts: Proportion
Compare and contrast the way that elements of visual art, dance, and music are used in a musical performance. Show students a scene from a musical, such as *Cats: The Musical*. Have them identify the way ideas and emotions are communicated through the relationships between visual elements, movement, and music. Compare and contrast the proportions of the visual elements with proportions of settings in real life.

Theatrical Arts Connection

Electronic Media Tell students that characters from film or television are often used in corresponding video or computer games. Have students view a computer game in which characters from a film interact in a setting. Have them describe elements of the game's setting.

Film Show an excerpt from the film that inspired the computer game used in **Electronic Media** above. Have students compare and contrast the setting of the film with the setting from the computer game. Based on the reasons students would prefer to view each version of these characters, have them compare the roles of electronic media and film in American society.

Standards

National Theatre Standard: The student understands context by recognizing the role of theatre, film, television, and electronic media in daily life.

Reflect

Time: About 10 minutes

Assessment

▶ Have students evaluate their participation by completing the **Unit 5 Self-Criticism Questions** on page 104.

▶ Use the assessment rubric to evaluate the students' participation in the **Unit Activity** and to assess their understanding of visual elements.

▶ Have students complete the **Unit 5 Quick Quiz** on page 105.

	3 Points	2 Points	1 Point
Perception	Has mastered concepts related to visual elements and can fully connect them with settings and clothing in real life.	Is developing an understanding of concepts related to visual elements and can somewhat connect them with settings and clothing in real life.	Has a minimal understanding of the concepts related to visual elements and has trouble connecting them with settings and clothing in real life.
Creative Expression	Participates fully in designing, creating, or selecting all of the following: props, makeup, costumes, and scenery. Uses all visual elements safely in the improvisation.	Participates fully in designing, creating, or selecting three of the following: props, makeup, costumes, and scenery. Uses all visual elements safely in the improvisation.	Participates fully in designing, creating, or selecting two of the following: props, makeup, costumes, and scenery. Does not use all visual elements safely in the improvisation.
History and Culture	Writes a paragraph clearly describing ways animals communicate and compares these with three ways animals communicate in "Animal Language." Clearly explains how he or she can use real-life observations.	Writes a paragraph describing ways animals communicate and compares these with two ways animals communicate in "Animal Language." Adequately explains how he or she can use real-life observations.	Writes a paragraph describing ways animals communicate and compares these with one way animals communicate in "Animal Language." Minimally explains how he or she can use real-life observations.
Evaluation	Thoughtfully and honestly evaluates own participation using the four steps of art criticism.	Attempts to evaluate own participation, but shows an incomplete understanding of evaluation criteria.	The student makes a minimal attempt to evaluate own participation.

Apply

▶ Discuss the ways people in theatre, including actors, designers, and playwrights, use observations of real life. *(Actors may look at the way people act in real life, and so on)*

▶ Have students think about what it is like eating lunch at school. Have them discuss the visual elements of the room and the people. Ask them to imagine it as a scene from a play and have volunteers give details about the setting, props, and costumes.

View a Performance

Visual Elements in Dance

▶ Have students identify and discuss aspects of appropriate audience behavior. Remind them to listen and watch the performance quietly and that an audience's job is being respectful of the performers and other audience members.

▶ If you have the *Artsource®* videocassette or DVD, have students view *Danza de la Reata* (Rope Dance) performed by Ballet Folklorico de Mexico; alternatively, you may have them view another Mexican folk dance. Explain that a *reata* is a rope used to tie horses or mules together to keep them moving in a straight line. In this dance, inspired by the Mexican dance style of *Mestizo*, the dancer uses the rope as a lariat, or lasso.

▶ Discuss the performance with students using the following questions:

Describe What visual elements did you see in this dance? *(a rope that is a prop, a hat and traditional costumes)* Describe the music. *(upbeat, trumpets playing, and so on)*

Analyze How did the props and costumes enhance the dancers' movements? *(The rope made the man's dance more interesting; the woman held her full, ruffled skirts.)*

Interpret Compare and contrast the feeling created by the music, costumes, and movement with the feeling created by the visual elements and movement you used in the **Activity**. How might an artist create the same feeling in an artwork?

Decide Do you think this dance might work well in some type of play? Why?

> "When a performance is over, what remains? . . . It is the play's central image that remains, its silhouette, and if the elements are rightly blended this silhouette will be its meaning, this shape will be the essence of what it has to say."
>
> —Peter Brook
> (1925-), director

LEARN ABOUT CAREERS IN THEATRE

Discuss the role of a set (sometimes called "scenic") designer in a play. Say, "The aim of a set designer is to give the set a look that matches the feeling and intention of the play. A set designer does not build real rooms in houses; instead, he or she might create the illusion of a room in the minds of audience members using painted canvas that is stretched over wood frames, realistic looking props made out of materials such as papier-maché or wood, and special effects." Discuss the ways a set designer must take into account other people's designs and intentions, such as making sure his or her setting works well with the costume designer's costumes or making sure the complexity of the setting fits a production's budget. Have students compare the work of a set designer with the work of a playwright.

Standards

National Theatre Standard: The student identifies and describes the visual, aural, oral, and kinetic elements of classroom dramatizations and dramatic performances.

Lesson 6 • Unit Activity

Name _____ Date _____

Unit 5 Self-Criticism Questions

Think about how you showed visual elements in your improvisation. Then answer the questions below.

1. **Describe** How did you use classroom items as props? Describe your makeup and costume designs. How did you help make the scenery?

   _____
   _____

2. **Analyze** How did you use your props when you acted as the doctor or a horse? How did your makeup and costume affect the way you moved and spoke as your animal character?

   _____
   _____

3. **Interpret** What would the visual elements show to an audience? How are they like or unlike doctor's offices and animals in real life?

   _____
   _____

4. **Decide** If you performed this improvisation again, would you change anything about your makeup, costume, or prop choices? Why or why not?

   _____
   _____

Name _____ Date _____

Unit 5 Quick Quiz

Completely fill in the bubble of the best answer for each question below.

1. **An example of a visual element is**
   - (A) the sound of a band playing music.
   - (B) something a character says.
   - (C) a chair in which characters sit onstage.
   - (D) none of the above.

2. **A mask is**
   - (F) always created through makeup.
   - (G) an element of sound.
   - (H) placed over an actor's face.
   - (J) not a visual element.

3. **Scenery, costumes, and props can show**
   - (A) setting.
   - (B) mood.
   - (C) character traits.
   - (D) all of the above.

4. **A personal prop is**
   - (F) an object used by an actor.
   - (G) a type of makeup.
   - (H) any object that is found onstage.
   - (J) the setting of a play.

5. **An example of scenery is**
   - (A) a door onstage.
   - (B) screens painted to look like a wall.
   - (C) a backdrop onstage that looks like the ocean.
   - (D) all of the above.

Score _____ (Top Score 5)

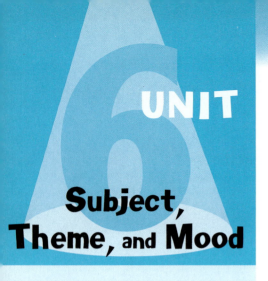

UNIT 6
Subject, Theme, and Mood

Lesson 1 • Subject, Theme, and the Five Ws The five *W*s help identify a play's subject and theme. *Tableau*

Lesson 2 • Finding Theme Theme can be determined by a thorough examination of subject. *Dramatic Movement*

Lesson 3 • Showing Mood Visual elements can help show mood. *Costumes*

Lesson 4 • A Director Shows Theme A director must make sure that all parts of a play communicate a unified theme. *Improvisation*

Lesson 5 • Actors Can Show Mood Body language and facial expressions are one way actors help create mood. *Tableau*

Lesson 6 • Unit Activity: Scripted Play This activity will give students the opportunity to write a script using elements of subject, theme, and mood.

See pages T3–T20 for more about **Theatre Technique Tips.**

Introduce Unit Concepts

"Subject and theme relate to a play's meaning. All elements of a production help communicate subject and theme, and they also work together to create mood, or emotional atmosphere." *"El sujeto y el tema relacionan con el mensaje o significado de un drama. Todos los elementos de una producción ayudan a comunicar sujeto y tema y también trabajan juntos para crear talante o ambiente emocional."*

Subject, Theme, and Mood

▶ Explain that in literature a story's subject is what happens to whom, but in theatre a play's subject is more abstract. It is the answer to the question, "What is this story about?" A theme of a play is the playwright's attitude toward the subject; if a play's subject is "good versus evil," a theme might be "good always wins over evil."

▶ Discuss the way visual elements in real life create mood, such as the effect of bright sunshine outside.

Vocabulary

Discuss the following vocabulary words.

subject *sujeto*—usually an abstract concept, such as fear or power; it answers the question, "What is this play about?"

theme *tema*—the attitude toward a subject communicated through a play's action

mood *talante*—the emotional atmosphere of a scene

Unit Links

Visual Arts: Balance, Harmony, Variety, and Unity
▶ Explain that the variety of actions, music, and dialogue in formal and informal theatre should communicate subject and theme. Similarly, both harmony, created through similar elements such as shape or color, and variety, created through diverse elements, work to create unity in artwork. Compare this with the way elements in dance and music may create unity.

▶ Show students the image of a painting, such as *The Concert* by Judith Leyster. Discuss the painting's balance, or visual weight. Discuss how students could dramatize the painting in a way that shows subject and balance.

Reading Theme: A Changing America
▶ Have students share events and people they associate with the early history of America, such as Christopher Columbus or the Boston Tea Party. Explain that America was built by many different groups of people.

▶ Discuss the American Revolution. Say, "A play about the revolution could have the subject of freedom. What theme might the play have?" *(Freedom comes at a cost, and so on.)*

Teacher Background

Background on Subject, Theme, and Mood

The subject of a play is more comparable to theme in literature; it deals with what the play is "about" in a larger sense. Examples of subjects for plays include *courage* and *good against evil.* Theme, then, is the attitude toward the subject conveyed through a play's action. For example, if the subject is *revenge,* the theme could be, "revenge is not satisfying." Most plays have several possible subjects and themes. A play's mood relates to subject and theme; for example, a scene about revenge probably would not have a light, happy mood.

Background on Directing

Although a director may work with a dramaturge when interpreting a script he or she must make the final decision. When deciding on subject and theme, a director may also consider a playwright's other works, the playwright's intentions (if known), the time period in which a play was written, and critical responses to past productions.

Research in Theatre Education

"The research showed that children in drama and arts classrooms improved in their self-confidence and self-concept, in their perception and self-awareness, in their thinking styles and self-expression, and in their motivation and transference of knowledge and experience—which varied with maturation."

—Richard Courtney

"A Lifetime of Drama Teaching and Research," in *Building Moral Communities through Educational Drama.*

Differentiated Instruction

Reteach
Have students name two different movies they have seen. Have them compare and contrast each movie's overall mood.

Challenge
Have students choose a subject, such as "freedom," and have them each think of a theme that could relate to this subject. Have them improvise scenes that illustrate each theme.

Special Needs
Students with certain attention disorders, such as ADHD or ADD, may have difficulty focusing during less structured activities. Make adaptations for this by discussing and displaying rules for each activity, providing as much structure in the physical space as possible, and using quick transactions between activities.

Theatre's Effects Across the Curriculum

★ **Reading/Writing**
Writing Comprehension Journal and script writing provide students with various opportunities to express, record, develop, and reflect ideas in a variety of ways.

★ **Math**
Application When students create an improvisation with a specific subject, mood, or theme, they must translate this information into character speech and action.

★ **Science**
Cause and Effect Studying how color and other design elements affect a production's mood gives students another opportunity to think about cause and effect.

★ **Social Studies**
History Improvisations that use historical subject matter give students the opportunity to use knowledge of history to explore situations.

★ **Music**
Friendship and Cooperation Students must apply cooperation skills when working as actors or musicians in an ensemble; both actors and musicians often form strong friendships as they work together to perfect performances.

★ **Dance**
Trust Just as students learn to trust each other as they perform a drama, so also dancers must trust each other in order to move in unison and cross paths in space as they travel.

Objectives

 Perception To identify ways the five Ws can help identify a play's subject and theme

 Creative Expression To create a tableau showing subject and theme

 History and Culture To identify subjects associated with dance and music of a Native American group in their region

 Evaluation To informally evaluate one's own work

Materials

- Copies of **"Subject, Theme, and the Five Ws" Warm-Up,** p. 109
- Journals or writing paper

Vocabulary

subject
theme

Standards

National Theatre Standard: The student is expected to identify and compare similar characters and situations in stories and dramas from and about various cultures, illustrate with classroom dramatizations, and discuss how theatre reflects life.

Listening/Speaking Standard: The student is expected to interact with peers in a variety of situations to develop and present familiar ideas (for example, conversations, whole group interactions, discussions).

Writing Standard: The student is expected to write to inform such as to explain, describe, report, and narrate.

Lesson 1: Subject, Theme and the Five Ws

Focus
Time: About 10 minutes

"In this lesson we will create a tableau to show subject and theme." *(See page T7 for more about Tableau.)*

Activate Prior Knowledge

▶ Remind students that a play's subject is different than a book's subject; it is usually an abstract idea, such as "fear." The five Ws of a play can help a director decide upon one possible subject. Remind students that the theme is a playwright's attitude toward that subject.

▶ Hand out the **"Subject, Theme, and the Five Ws" Warm-Up,** and have students complete it. Discuss their answers. As a class decide on a subject, theme, and set of five Ws for the **Warm-Up** image.

Teach
Time: About 15 minutes

Prepare Divide students into two groups.

Lead

▶ Tell students to create a tableau of what might happen next after the scene on the **Warm-Up,** based on the subject, theme, and five Ws they selected as a class.

▶ Allow time for planning, emphasizing that they should think about the five Ws of the situation.

▶ Have each group form its tableau, and have one member say its theme in the form of a sentence as students stand frozen. Discuss and replay.

Informal Assessment Did each tableau depict subject, theme, and the five Ws?

 History and Culture

Explain that when European explorers came to the Americas, the Native Americans who already lived there had a rich theatrical tradition of dance and music. Have students research arts traditions of local or regional Native American groups. Discuss the five Ws of related festivals and identify subjects associated with these traditions.

Reflect
Time: About 5 minutes

▶ Have students compare and contrast the tableaux.

Apply

Journal: Identifying
Have students imagine that a play is to be made about a time in their own lives when they experienced change; in their journals have them identify the play's five Ws, subject, and theme.

Name _____ Date _____

Subject, Theme, and the Five Ws

Look at the picture below. It shows Spanish explorers coming to America. Imagine you will be making a play about this story.

On the lines below, describe the five Ws of this scene.

_____
_____
_____
_____
_____

Circle the subject and theme that you will explore in your play.

Subjects	**Themes**
Trouble	"Misunderstandings lead to trouble."
	"People bring trouble on themselves."
Friendship	"Friendship has to be worked for."
	"Friendship is a gift."

Unit 6 • **Subject, Theme, and Mood**   Lesson 1 • Subject, Theme, and the Five Ws

Objectives

Perception To explore a poem in preparation for identifying theme

Creative Expression To use dramatic movement in response to a poem and use the movement to identify a theme

History and Culture To identify common themes in American theatrical works

Evaluation To informally evaluate one's own work

Materials

- Copies of "Finding Theme" Warm-Up, p. 111
- Journals or writing paper

Vocabulary

theme

Standards

National Theatre Standard: The student is expected to assume roles that exhibit concentration and contribute to the action of classroom dramatizations based on personal experience and heritage, imagination, literature, and history.

Listening/Speaking Standard: The student uses listening strategies effectively.

Reading Standard: The student is expected to read classic and contemporary works.

Lesson 2: Finding Theme

Focus
Time: About 10 minutes

"In this lesson we will interpret a poem to show its theme." *(See page T13 for more about Dramatic Movement.)*

Activate Prior Knowledge

▶ Hand out the **"Finding Theme" Warm-Up.** Discuss with students any unfamiliar words and careers, such as *melodious* or *deckhand*. Read the poem aloud while students use narrative pantomime to show its actions.

▶ Discuss the different careers and people described in the poem.

Teach
Time: About 15 minutes

Prepare Divide students into two groups.

Lead

▶ Have one group divide up the lines in the poem and plan a choral reading of it. The other group should divide the actions from the poem, allowing groups of students to represent each person from the poem.

▶ Have the second group safely perform their dramatic movements while the first group performs their choral reading. If time allows, have groups switch roles and replay.

▶ Discuss the five *W*s, possible subjects (such as *work*) and possible themes (such as, "America is created by its citizens' hard work.")

Informal Assessment Did each student participate in the reading and/or dramatic movement?

History and Culture

Discuss the way that popular themes in theatre, movies, and other dramatic presentations reflect culture. Explain that a culture's beliefs about people and life affect the theatre it produces. Ask, "What American ideas are communicated through this poem? What types of ideas are important in the history of America?" *(the importance of hard work and freedom)* Discuss the role of live theatre, film, and television in America as communicators of such cultural ideals.

Reflect
Time: About 5 minutes

▶ Discuss other themes students can identify in their dramatization.

Apply

Journal: Creative Writing
Have each student write a poem from the point of view of the role they portrayed in the poem, focusing on a new theme.

Unit 6 • Subject, Theme, and Mood

Finding Theme

I Hear America Singing

by Walt Whitman

I hear America singing, the varied carols I hear,

Those of mechanics, each one singing his as it should be blithe and strong,

The carpenter singing his as he measures his plank or beam,

The mason singing his as he makes ready for work, or leaves off work,

The boat man singing what belongs to him in his boat, the deckhand singing on the steamboat deck,

The shoemaker singing as he sits on his bench, the hatter singing as he stands,

The wood-cutter's song, the plowboy's on his way in the morning, or at noon intermission, or at sundown,

The delicious singing of the mother, or of the young wife at work, or of the girl sewing or washing,

Each singing what belongs to him or her and to none else,

The day what belongs to the day—at night the party of young fellows, robust, friendly,

Singing with open mouths their strong melodious songs.

Objectives

Perception To identify ways color in visual elements can show mood

Creative Expression To design costumes that evoke mood

History and Culture To identify genres of movies that create certain moods

Evaluation To informally evaluate one's own work

Materials

- Copies of "Showing Mood" Warm-Up, p. 113
- Drawing paper and colored pencils
- Various scraps of fabric
- Journals or writing paper

Vocabulary

mood

Unit Links

Visual Arts: Harmony
Compare and contrast the use of harmony in theatre and art. Explain that the use of similar colors or shapes in an artwork can create harmony; artists might use bright colors to create harmony while also creating a cheerful mood. Discuss with students other places they could use the colors from their costumes in a theatrical production. *(scenery, programs, and so on)*

Standards

National Theatre Standard: The student is expected to select movement, music, or visual elements to enhance the mood of a classroom dramatization.

Listening/Speaking Standard: The student uses listening strategies effectively.

Fine Arts/Visual Arts Standard: The student is expected to design original artworks.

Lesson 3: Showing Mood

Focus
Time: About 10 minutes

"In this lesson we will design costumes to show mood." *(See page T18 for more about Costumes.)*

Activate Prior Knowledge

▶ Hand out the **"Showing Mood" Warm-Up,** and have students complete it.

▶ Explain to students that one way visual elements can create mood is through color. Usually scenery and costumes with bright colors reflect a happy mood suitable for a light comedy; a darkened room in shades of gray would communicate a sad or serious mood.

Teach
Time: About 15 minutes

Prepare Divide students into pairs.

Lead

▶ Have each pair brainstorm ideas for characters and a play about a reunion that matches the mood from the **Warm-Up.** They should use real-life events as the basis for their story ideas.

▶ Have each pair design costumes for two characters in their play, using color and the style of their costumes to show the mood.

▶ Tell students that costume designers often include small pieces of fabric that would be used in the costume. Have each pair choose a scrap of fabric, use the fabric's pattern within their design, and attach the piece of fabric to the bottom of their design. Have pairs share their costumes with the class.

Informal Assessment Did each group's costumes match the appropriate mood?

 History and Culture

Explain to students that there are different types of movies that inspire different emotions. Discuss genres, such as comedy, drama, suspense, and horror. Ask students what emotions each type creates. *(Comedy might create a mood of fun, while horror will inspire feelings of fear, and so on.)* Discuss how costumes in each genre can help create mood.

Reflect
Time: About 5 minutes

▶ Have students identify each pair's mood; have pairs explain what mood they intended to express.

Apply

Journal: Describing
Have students write in their journals how a certain movie made them feel and describe how the visual elements added to the mood of the movie.

Name _____ Date _____

Showing Mood

Look at the picture below. What mood does it create?

In the box below, draw a memory that shows the same mood.

Unit 6 • **Subject, Theme, and Mood** Lesson 3 • Showing Mood

Objectives

 Perception To identify ways a director can show theme

 Creative Expression To direct others in an improvisation that shows theme

 History and Culture To learn about the Lost Colony and identify possible themes for a dramatization of this story

 Evaluation To informally evaluate one's own work

Materials

❍ Items for use as props, costume pieces, and scenic elements, such as pieces of fabric, chairs, hats, and so on

❍ Journals or writing paper

Unit Links

Visual Arts: Unity
Unity and theme are linked in art and theatre. Explain to students that an artist can show a central theme by using all elements in an artwork to create unity. Tell students that directors combine visual, verbal, musical, and movement elements to create a unified presentation of a play's theme. Have each student create a drawing of a scene from his or her improvisation that communicates its theme.

Standards

National Theatre Standard: The student directs by planning classroom dramatizations.

Listening/Speaking Standard: The student listens and speaks both to gain and share knowledge of his/her own culture, the culture of others, and the common elements of cultures.

Social Studies Standard: The student understands the causes and effects of European exploration and colonization of the Western Hemisphere.

114

Lesson 4: A Director Shows Theme

Focus
Time: About 10 minutes

"In this lesson we will direct improvisations to show theme." *(See page T4 for more about Improvisation.)*

Activate Prior Knowledge

▶ Discuss how a director uses theme. He or she first identifies it (often with the help of others), and then works with designers and actors to communicate this theme.

Teach
Time: About 15 minutes

Prepare Divide students into groups of three.

Lead Read aloud **"The Mystery of Roanoke Island."** Say, "We are going to improvise what might have happened to the Lost Colony. Decide what you think might have happened to them. Choose a subject, theme, and mood based on your idea."

▶ Have each group assign roles, such as Eleanor Dare (mother of Virginia) or Chief Manteo of the Croatoans, and choose a director. Explain that the director and actors must work together on the improvisation; the director should only make changes to better show the theme.

▶ Have students safely incorporate props, costumes, and any scenic elements to help define the characters, their actions, and the theme as they improvise. Have each student take a turn as director.

Informal Assessment Did each student work as a director and/or with a director to show theme?

 History and Culture

Explain that the Lost Colony is a great mystery. Some people think the colonists went to live with Native Americans. One explorer later claimed that some of the Croatoan tribe had grey eyes and could read. In the 1880s, some Pembroke Native Americans of North Carolina said their ancestors came from "Roanoke in Virginia." If possible, have students research the Lost Colony on the Internet. Discuss possible themes for dramatizations, such as "good intentions are not enough for a colony to succeed."

Reflect
Time: About 5 minutes

▶ Have students describe how each theme was supported through the characters, their relationships, and their surroundings.

Apply

 Journal: Explaining
Have students identify in their journals a possible theme for another story from history, using facts to support their choice.

Unit 6 • **Subject, Theme, and Mood**

The Mystery of Roanoke Island

from *American History Stories, Volume I* by Mara L. Pratt

England was very anxious to get a colony founded in North America. Several attempts were made, but none of them were successful. One colony, called in history "The Lost Colony," was made up of a hundred families. They settled upon the beautiful island of Roanoke in Albemarle Sound, Virginia.

When their rough houses were built and the people had planted their fields and seemed comfortable and prosperous, their governor, John Whyte, returned to England to report their success and to bring back provisions for the colony.

The governor did not like to leave the colony. His people depended on him for guidance, and then, too, there was a little baby girl, his granddaughter—little Virginia Dare, the first English baby born on American soil. But the colonists needed provisions, so the brave governor sailed away.

On reaching England he found the country in such commotion and the queen so busy with the war going on between Spain and England, that it was three long years before he could get together the provisions and the help he needed to carry back to the little colony.

When at last he did set sail, it seemed to him that the ocean must have grown thousands and thousands of miles wider, the voyage was so long and he was so anxious about the little colony.

At last the vessel neared the island. Eagerly Governor Whyte looked up and down the shores for some sign of welcome. But only the stillness and the gloom of the forest greeted him. Not a sign of life. The huts were deserted, not a sound was to be heard save the cry of the birds and the moaning of the trees.

On a tree were cut the letters, CROATOAN. What did that mean? Was it the name of some place to which the colonists had moved? No one knew. No one ever knew; and not one trace of this lost colony, not one trace of the little English baby, Virginia Dare, has been found to this day.

Objectives

 Perception To identify ways characters can physically show mood

 Creative Expression To create a tableau that shows mood

 History and Culture To learn about one cause of the American Revolution

Evaluation To informally evaluate one's own work

Materials

- Copies of **"Actors Can Show Mood" Warm-Up,** p. 117
- Journals or writing paper

Vocabulary

theme
mood

Standard

National Theatre Standard: The student is expected to assume roles that exhibit concentration and contribute to the action of classroom dramatizations based on personal experience and heritage, imagination, literature, and history.

Listening/Speaking Standard: The student is expected to connect his/her own experiences, information, insights, and ideas with those of others through speaking and listening.

Writing Standard: The student writes for a variety of audiences and purposes, and in a variety of forms.

Lesson 5: Actors Can Show Mood

Focus
Time: About 10 minutes

"In this lesson we will create tableaux to show mood." *(See page T7 for more about Tableau.)*

Activate Prior Knowledge

▶ Hand out the **"Actors Can Show Mood" Warm-Up,** and have students complete it.

▶ Discuss students' answers, and have students imitate the facial expressions and body positions of the characters. Explain that actors in plays can help create mood through their speech and actions.

Teach
Time: About 15 minutes

Prepare Divide students into groups of three.

Lead Explain that the **Warm-Up** shows two of five laws made by the British that made colonists very angry. They called these laws the "Five Intolerable Acts;" *intolerable* meant that they were so bad that people could not live with them.

▶ Read the following aloud: "Another Intolerable Act took away many of Massachusetts' rights. People could not have town meetings, and they could not vote for the people in their government. Yet another act let British officers go back to England to be put on trial for crimes. The colonists knew this meant that the officers would probably not be punished."

▶ Have each student group choose one act. How might people have protested this act? Tell them to create a tableau to illustrate the way colonists worked for change, making sure to choose and show a mood.

Informal Assessment Did each group's tableau show mood?

 History and Culture

Explain that the Five Intolerable Acts were one thing that led to the American Revolution. The American Constitution includes laws protecting people's rights, such as Amendments that do not allow quartering of soldiers or that guarantee the right to have peaceful meetings. Discuss another Constitutional right, such as freedom of speech, and identify possible moods students associate with it.

Reflect
Time: About 5 minutes

▶ Have students compare and contrast the mood for each tableau.

Apply

 Journal: Inferring
Have students write a journal entry describing how they would feel if they had to let soldiers from another country stay in their homes.

Name _____   Date _____

Actors Can Show Mood

Warm-Up

One reason for the American Revolution was that colonists did not think the British government treated them fairly. The pictures below show two problems people had.

1. **Quartering of Soldiers** Colonists had to let British soldiers stay in their homes. They had to give them food. This was called "quartering" soldiers. Colonists did not think this was fair.

2. **Closing the Harbor** People were angry about unfair taxes on tea. Some people put on disguises and threw a lot of tea into Boston Harbor. This was later called the Boston Tea Party. Because of this, England closed Boston Harbor. Many people could not work because the harbor was closed.

Describe the moods created by each picture on the lines below.

1. _____

2. _____

Unit 6 • Subject, Theme, and Mood   Lesson 5 • Actors Can Show Mood   117

Objectives

Perception To review elements of subject, theme, and mood and to connect these concepts to music and a script

Creative Expression To write and perform a script

History and Culture To perform research to be used in a script

Evaluation To thoughtfully and honestly evaluate one's own participation using the four steps of criticism

Materials

- Items for use as props, costume pieces, and scenic elements, such as pieces of fabric, chairs, hats, and so on
- Copies of the **Unit 6 Self-Criticism Questions**, p. 122
- Copies of the **Unit 6 Quick Quiz**, p. 123
- *Artsource*® Performing Arts Resource Package (optional)

Lesson 6 Unit Activity: Scripted Play

Focus

Time: About 10 minutes

Review Unit Concepts

"A subject of a play can be discovered by asking, 'What is this play about?' A theme is an opinion about the subject that is communicated through a play. Mood is the overall feeling of a play or scene." **"Se puede descubrir el sujeto de un drama haciendo la pregunta, '¿de qué se trata este drama?' Un tema es lo que dice un drama sobre un sujeto en particular. Todos los elementos de las producciones dramáticas trabajan juntos para crear talante."**

▶ Review with students the ways they explored subject, theme, and mood in this unit.

▶ Review the unit vocabulary on page 106.

 History and Culture

Have pairs of students (formed during the **First Rehearsal**) use a student-safe search engine, such as **www.yahooligans.com**, to research a European explorer, such as Cabeza de Vaca, Christopher Columbus, Francisco Coronado, Ponce de Leon, or Sieur de la Salle. Have pairs also research the Native American tribe(s) their explorer met first upon reaching the Americas. Tell them to use at least four specific details from their research in their scripts.

Classroom Management Tips

The following are tips for managing your classroom during the **Rehearsals** and Activity:

✔ **Emphasize Point of View** If students are struggling with how to approach their stories, encourage them to improvise the meeting between their explorer and the Native Americans twice—once from each group's point of view. Tell students that the theme and mood of their script will depend on whose point of view it is told from.

✔ **Engage in Role Playing** To help guide students who are struggling with their improvisation, join them in the improvisation and act as the interpreter or as the explorer.

✔ **Encourage Authenticity** Encourage students to be creative with their scripts, but to keep in mind the facts they learned from their research.

Standards

National Theatre Standard: The student is expected to communicate information to peers about people, events, time, and place related to classroom dramatizations.

Teach

Time: Two 25-minute rehearsal periods
One 35-minute activity period

First Rehearsal

▶ Divide students into pairs. Explain that each pair will write a short script depicting an encounter between a group of explorers and a group of Native Americans in early America.

▶ Have each group do research on the Internet to decide which group of explorers they would like to show (see **History and Culture**), and have them brainstorm ideas about how each group would feel. Remind them that the groups would not have spoken the same language, and so would need an interpreter or would have to communicate nonverbally.

▶ If time allows, have different pairs team up and improvise scenes based on each pair's script ideas. Alternatively, have each pair improvise scenes individually.

▶ Have each pair write a brief description of its script's characters, their relationships, their environment, and the mood of their scene, and have them turn these descriptions in to you for your review.

Second Rehearsal

▶ Have students re-form the pairs from the **First Rehearsal;** distribute their descriptions with your comments. Show students the example of a script on page 41 and have them use this when formatting their scripts. Explain that playwrights often include directions about movement or tone of voice in their scripts, often within parentheses. *(See page T10 for more about Script Writing.)*

▶ Have students write a simple script for their scene, incorporating your comments.

▶ Have groups of pairs team up and read each others' scripts aloud; have pairs make revisions based on these readings.

▶ Each pair should end by checking their script's spelling and grammar, and then should turn it in to you for your review.

Subject, Theme, and Mood Activity

▶ Have students re-form the pairs from the **Second Rehearsal;** distribute their scripts with your comments on them. Have the pairs look over your comments and make any final changes.

▶ Group several pairs into larger groups; have volunteers from each group plan and perform each pair's script, selecting and safely incorporating prop objects, costume pieces, and any other visual elements that might help show the theme.

▶ Have the class express which parts they liked about each script, as well as sharing any appropriate, constructive criticism. Discuss some subjects and themes from different scripts.

Standards

National Theatre Standard: The student is expected to improvise dialogue to tell stories, and formalize improvisations by writing or recording the dialogue.

Unit Links

Visual Arts: Balance
Balance can be used in theatre, art, and dance. Explain that the way scenic elements and props are balanced onstage can help create mood; for example, a play with a mood of confusion and disarray might have visual elements scattered across the stage. Compare and contrast this use of balance with the use of balance in artwork, which creates visual weight through the arrangement of elements such as shape and color. How might a choreographer use balance? *(He or she could arrange dancers onstage in a balanced way.)*

Theatrical Arts Connection

Electronic Media Discuss video games with which students are familiar, and have them identify the mood of each game. *(serious, silly, and so on)* Have students identify how visual elements create this mood. Even though they all have different moods, what is the role of such games in modern American society? *(entertainment, education)* How does the mood affect a game's entertainment value? *(Sometimes you want to play a game that seems realistic and intense, so you would want to play a game with a serious mood, and so on.)*

Film Discuss a popular movie with which students are familiar. Lead students in the process of identifying a possible subject and theme for this movie. Accept all probable answers if the students can support their opinions with specifics from the film.

Standards

National Theatre Standard: The student understands context by recognizing the role of theatre, film, television, and electronic media in daily life.

Reflect

Time: About 10 minutes

Assessment

▶ Have students evaluate their participation by completing the **Unit 6 Self-Criticism Questions** on page 122.

▶ Use the assessment rubric to evaluate the students' participation in the **Unit Activity** and to assess their understanding of subject, theme, and mood.

▶ Have students complete the **Unit 6 Quick Quiz** on page 123.

	3 Points	2 Points	1 Point
Perception	Gives full attention to review. Masters an understanding of the connection between mood and music and between subject, theme, and point of view.	Gives partial attention to review. Is developing an understanding of the connection between mood and music and between subject, theme, and point of view.	Gives minimal attention to review. Has a minimal understanding of the connection between mood and music and between subject, theme, and point of view.
Creative Expression	Fully participates in all of the following: prewriting, improvisation, drafting, revising, and performing.	Participates in four of the following: prewriting, improvisation, drafting, revising, and performing.	Participates in three of the following: prewriting, improvisation, drafting, revising, and performing.
History and Culture	Uses at least four specific details from the research in a script.	Uses three specific details from the research in a script.	Uses only one or two specific details from the research in a script.
Evaluation	Thoughtfully and honestly evaluates own participation using the four steps of art criticism.	Attempts to evaluate own participation, but shows an incomplete understanding of evaluation criteria.	Makes a minimal attempt to evaluate own participation.

Apply

▶ Discuss the music to which students like to listen. What sort of mood does it create? Would this music be useful in a theatrical production in which that same mood is being created? What are some reasons why it would or would not work in such a production?

▶ Discuss students' scripts from the **Activity**. How did point of view affect each script's subject and theme? Was the exploration of the New World exciting for one group of people? How did it create problems and challenges for each culture involved?

View a Performance

Subject, Mood, and Theme in Music

▶ Discuss with students aspects of appropriate audience behavior. Have students agree to apply this behavior while listening to the performance.

▶ If you have the *Artsource*® audiocassette or DVD, have students listen to "Jaropo Azul" by Alfredo Rolando Ortiz. Alternatively, have them listen to another recording of Paraguayan harp music. Have students show their responses to the music by using rhythmic movement and vocal sounds.

▶ Discuss the performance with students using the following questions:

Describe What kinds of sounds do you hear in this music? *(a harp repeating notes in patterns)*

Analyze What kind of movement would this music motivate? *(slow, repeated dance steps)* What kind of mood does the music create? *(peaceful, happy)*

Interpret Describe the plot of a play that would go well with this music. What might be the play's subject or theme? *(Answers will vary.)* How does the music create a rhythmic beat? Compare this use of rhythm with rhythmic elements in visual art and dance.

Decide Compare and contrast the music's feeling with the feeling created by the performance of your script.

"Every element in a staged play is part of its direction."

—Harold Clurman (1901–1980), director/theatre critic

LEARN ABOUT
CAREERS IN THEATRE

Ask students, "How does a director help demonstrate the subject, theme, and mood of a play?" *(working with actors and designers)* Explain that it was only in the late nineteenth century that the role of director came into existence; before that, an actor-manager usually hired and coached the actors. In modern professional theatre a director is hired by a producer, a person who handles the business side of play production. Modern directors must analyze a play and decide how one particular production is going to interpret its subject, theme, and moods. Have students compare the roles of director and actor, discussing the responsibilities of each.

Standards

National Theatre Standard: The student describes visual, aural, oral, and kinetic elements in theatre, dramatic media, dance, music, and visual arts.

Name _____ Date _____

Unit 6 Self-Criticism Questions

Think about how you wrote a script.
Then answer the questions below.

1. **Describe** Who were the characters in your script? From whose point of view was the script written? Describe the actions in your script.

   _____
   _____

2. **Analyze** What subject and theme did you choose for your script? How did you communicate the subject and theme? What mood did the performance of your script create?

   _____
   _____

3. **Interpret** Compare and contrast the way characters acted in your script with the way you have acted in unfamiliar situations.

   _____
   _____

4. **Decide** Would you change anything about your script? Why or why not?

   _____
   _____

Name _____ Date _____

Unit 6   Quick Quiz

Completely fill in the bubble of the best answer for each question below.

1. **The subject of a play answers the question,**
   - Ⓐ Why did the playwright write this play?
   - Ⓑ What might happen next?
   - Ⓒ What costumes should be used in this play?
   - Ⓓ What is this play about?

2. **Theme is the**
   - Ⓕ attitude toward a subject shown through a play's action.
   - Ⓖ attitude of a director toward a play's actors.
   - Ⓗ characters in a play.
   - Ⓙ feeling of a play.

3. **Mood is**
   - Ⓐ a feeling created by a play.
   - Ⓑ the lighting on a set.
   - Ⓒ the director of a play.
   - Ⓓ not important in theatre.

4. **A director's job is**
   - Ⓕ working with actors to create mood.
   - Ⓖ deciding on a subject and theme for a play.
   - Ⓗ working with designers to create mood.
   - Ⓙ all of the above.

5. **Which of the following is *not* true?**
   - Ⓐ Costumes can help create mood.
   - Ⓑ A subject of a play could be *honesty*.
   - Ⓒ Scenery cannot create mood.
   - Ⓓ Directors help actors show theme.

Score _____ (Top Score 5)

Unit 6 • **Subject, Theme, and Mood**   Lesson 6 • Unit Activity

Adventure in the Wild Wood

from *The Wind in the Willows*
by Kenneth Grahame (Adapted)

When cautious, friendly Mole leaves his home at Mole End one spring, his whole world changes when he meets kind, boat-loving Rat and boastful Toad of Toad Hall. Mole wants to go into the Wild Wood to meet the Badger, a friend of Rat's, even though Rat has warned him that the Wild Wood is too dangerous. One afternoon when Rat is sleeping, Mole sneaks out and enters the Wild Wood.

There was nothing to alarm Mole at first entry. Twigs crackled under his feet, logs tripped him, funguses on stumps looked like caricatures, and startled him for the moment by their likeness to something familiar and far away; but that was all fun and exciting. It led him on, and he went to where the light was less, and trees crouched nearer and nearer, and holes made ugly mouths at him on either side.

Everything was very still now. The dusk advanced on him steadily, rapidly, gathering in behind and before; and the light seemed to be draining away like floodwater.

Then the faces began.

It was over his shoulder, and indistinctly, that he first thought he saw a face; a little evil wedge-shaped face, looking out at him from a hole. When he turned and confronted it, the thing had vanished.

He quickened his pace, telling himself cheerfully not to begin imagining things, or there would be simply no end to it. He passed another hole, and another, and another; and then—yes!—no!—yes! Certainly a little narrow face with hard eyes had flashed up for an instant from a hole, and was gone. He hesitated—braced himself up for an effort and strode on. Then suddenly, and as if it had been so all the time, every hole, far and near, and there were hundreds of them, seemed to possess its face, coming and going rapidly, all fixing on him glances of malice and hatred: all hard-eyed and evil and sharp.

If he could only get away from the holes in the banks, he thought, there would be no more faces. He swung off the path and plunged into the untrodden places of the wood.

Then the whistling began.

Very faint and shrill it was, and far behind him, when first he heard it; but somehow it made him hurry forward. Then, still very faint and shrill, it sounded far ahead of him, and made him hesitate and want to go back. As he halted in indecision it broke out on either side, and seemed to be caught up and passed on throughout the whole length of the wood to its farthest limit. They were up and alert and ready, evidently, whoever they were! And he—he was alone, and unarmed, and far from any help; and the night was closing in.

Then the pattering began.

The pattering increased till it sounded like sudden hail on the dry leaf-carpet spread around him. The whole wood seemed running now, running hard, hunting, chasing, closing in round something or—somebody? In panic, he began to run, too, aimlessly, he knew not whither. He ran up against things, he fell over things and into things, he darted under things and dodged round things. At last he took refuge in the deep dark hollow of an old beech tree, which offered shelter, concealment—perhaps even safety, but who could tell? Anyhow, he was too tired to run any further, and could only snuggle down into the dry leaves which had drifted into the hollow and hope he was safe for a time. And as he lay there panting and trembling, and listened to the whistlings and the patterings outside, he knew it at last, in all its fullness, that dread thing which other little dwellers in field and hedgerow had encountered here, and known as their darkest moment—that thing which the Rat had vainly tried to shield him from—the Terror of the Wild Wood!

Meantime the Rat, warm and comfortable, dozed by his fireside. His paper of half-finished verses slipped from his knee, his head fell back, his mouth opened, and he wandered by the verdant banks of dream-rivers. Then a coal slipped, the fire crackled and sent up a spurt of flame, and he woke with a start. Remembering what he had been reading, he reached down to the floor for his verses, looked over them for a minute, and then looked round for the Mole to ask him if he knew a good rhyme for something or other.

But the Mole was not there.

He listened for a time. The house seemed very quiet.

Then he called "Moly!" several times, and, hearing no answer, got up and went out into the hall.

The Mole's cap was missing from its peg. His boots, which always lay by the umbrella-stand, were also gone.

The Rat left the house and carefully examined the muddy surface of the ground outside, hoping to find the Mole's tracks. There they were, sure enough. The boots were new, just bought for the winter, and the dimples on their soles were fresh and sharp. He could see the imprints of them in the mud, running along straight and purposeful, leading direct to the Wild Wood.

The Rat looked very grave and stood in deep thought for a minute or two. Then he reentered the house, strapped a belt round his waist, shoved a brace of pistols into it, took up a stout club that stood in a corner of the hall, and set off for the Wild Wood at a smart pace.

It was already getting toward dusk when he reached the first fringe of trees and plunged without hesitation into the wood, looking anxiously on either side for any sign of his friend. Here and there wicked little faces popped out of holes, but vanished immediately at the sight of the brave animal, his pistols, and the great ugly club in his grasp; and the whistling and pattering, which he had heard quite plainly on his first entry, died away and ceased, and all was very still. He made his way manfully through the length of the wood to its furthest edge; then, forsaking all paths, he set himself to cross it, and all the time calling out cheerfully, "Moly, Moly, Moly! Where are you? It's me—it's old Rat!"

He had patiently hunted through the wood for an hour or more, when at last to his joy he heard a little answering cry. Guiding himself by the sound, he made his way through the gathering darkness to the foot of an old beech tree, with a hole in it, and from out of the hole came a feeble voice, saying, "Ratty! Is that really you?"

The Rat crept into the hollow, and there he found the Mole, exhausted and still trembling. "O Rat!" he cried, "I've been so frightened, you can't think!"

"O, I quite understand," said the Rat soothingly. "You shouldn't really have gone and done it, Mole. I did my best to keep you from it. We river-bankers, we hardly ever come here by ourselves. If we have to come, we come in couples, at least; then we're generally all right. Besides, there are a hundred things one has to know, which we understand all about and you don't, as yet. I mean passwords, and signs, and sayings which have power and effect, and plants you carry in your pocket, and verses you repeat, and dodges and tricks you practice; all simple enough when you know them, but they've got to be known if you're small, or you'll find yourself in trouble. Of course if you were Badger or Otter, it would be quite another matter."

"Surely the brave Mr. Toad wouldn't mind coming here by himself, would he?" inquired the Mole.

"Old Toad?" said the Rat, laughing heartily. "He wouldn't show his face here alone, not for a whole hatful of golden coins, Toad wouldn't."

The Mole was greatly cheered by the sound of the Rat's careless laughter, as well as by the sight of his stick and his gleaming pistols, and he stopped shivering and began to feel bolder and more himself again.

"Now then," said the Rat presently, "we really must pull ourselves together and make a start for home while there's still a little light left."

Name _____ Date _____

The Barber's Clever Wife
a tale from India

Activity Story

Once there was a barber who was very handsome, very charming, and very lazy. Every time Alok the barber made a few pennies cutting hair, he would spend the money before he ever came home. So of course he grew poorer every day, till at last he and his wife were left with nothing but their house.

Manisha, the barber's clever wife, was angry with her lazy husband. "Go and beg for something from the king," she said. "It is his wedding feast; he will give gifts to the poor."

"Very well," said Alok. He was afraid of his smart wife, so he went to the palace and begged the king to give him something.

"Something?" asked the king. "*What* thing?"

Before he knew what he was saying, the silly barber said, "Give me a piece of wasteland outside the city."

So the king ordered a piece of this useless land to be given to Alok the barber.

Manisha was furious when Alok came home. "Why on earth did you not ask for some money to buy food?!" she said.

"Land is land!" said Alok. "We will always have it!"

"Land is only good if you can grow food on it," his wife said, "and we do not have a plow to dig up our land." But Manisha began to think, and soon she had a plan.

The next day Manisha took Alok to their land. "Look at the ground like I do. Do not ask why," she told him. Manisha and Alok walked around all day, looking carefully at the dirt.

Seven robbers were hiding nearby, and they watched the barber and his wife all day long. At sunset one robber said to the others, "I will find out what they are looking for," and he went to Manisha.

"Hello," he said. "Are you looking for something?"

Manisha leaned toward the robber and whispered, "My grandfather hid five pots of gold in this land. We are looking for the right place to dig for the gold. But do not tell anyone!"

"It is our secret," the robber said, and then he ran back to the other robbers. "That field has five pots of hidden gold," he told them. "We will dig them up tonight!"

When Manisha and the barber went home, the robbers began to dig. They dug up every bit of the ground, but they never found even one gold coin. By morning the ground looked like it had been plowed seven times, and Manisha laughed when she saw it. She and her husband borrowed some seed

Unit 2 • **Character**

Lesson 6 • Unit Activity

and planted it in their land. They grew rice and sold it for piles of money.

The robbers were very mad. They knew they had been tricked, so they made a plan to steal Manisha and Alok's money. They hid near the barber's house so they could find out where Alok and Manisha had hidden their money.

Manisha saw one of the robbers hiding near her window, and she decided to trick him. "Alok," she said to her husband, "I just want you to know that I hid all our money in the *nîm* tree outside. No one will look for it there!" The robbers heard her and thought, "Aha!" So that night the robbers went to the *nîm* tree.

"I see the gold," one robber said. "I will climb up the tree." But what he really saw was a big hornet's nest, full of big, yellow hornets.

As he climbed up the tree, a hornet stung him on his leg. He slapped at his leg.

"You are putting the gold in your own pocket," the robbers on the ground said. "We can see your hand on your pocket!"

"No, no," the robber in the tree whispered back. "Something is biting me!" Just then another hornet stung him, and he slapped his leg again.

One by one the robbers climbed up the tree after him, saying, "He is putting some money in his pocket!" The hornets began to sting all of them, and they all slapped at their legs and arms. Suddenly the branch with the hornet's nest broke, and the nest fell on top of the robbers. "Ahhh!" they all cried, falling from the tree.

After this the barber's wife had some peace, for all seven robbers were in the hospital. They were gone so long that Manisha thought they would never come back. But she was wrong, for one hot summer night the robbers returned. The barber and his wife were sleeping outside because the house was too hot. The robbers snuck up, picked up Manisha's mattress, and carried her off while she was fast asleep.

When Manisha woke up, she realized what had happened. How could she get away? The robbers carried her for a long time, but when they were tired, they stopped under a banyan tree. Quick as lightning, Manisha grabbed a tree branch and pulled herself into the tree, leaving her blanket on the bed just as if she were still in it.

"Let us rest here," said the robbers who were carrying the bed. "We are tired. She is so heavy!"

The barber's wife almost laughed, but she kept still. Soon the robbers began to argue about who would keep watch while the others slept. The robber captain finally said he would, and the others went to sleep.

Manisha had an idea. She pulled her white veil over her face and began to sing. The robber captain looked up and saw a strange woman in the tree. "It is some kind of tree fairy!" he said to himself. "She must be in love with me!" So he twirled his moustache, and walked around, waiting for her to speak. Finally he called out, "Come down, my beauty! I won't hurt you!" But Manisha only sighed.

"What is the matter?" he asked. "Of course you are a fairy who is in love with me, but that is no reason to sigh!"

"You do not really love me," Manisha said.

"No, I do. I do!" the robber captain cried.

"You are lying," Manisha said. "If you really love me, you will climb up this tree and let me kiss you."

The robber captain scrambled up the tree as fast as he could, but Manisha began to yell and shake the tree branches. The captain slipped and fell—bump, bump, bump!—down to the ground.

The other robbers woke up. "What happened?" they cried, but the robber captain had been knocked out by the fall.

"There, up in the tree!" one robber said, pointing at Manisha. "It's some kind of monster!" The robbers ran away as fast as they could, dragging their captain with them. They were so terrified they never came back to that city again.

Manisha smiled to herself. She climbed down the tree, put her mattress on her head, and quietly carried it home.

The Story of Susan La Flesche Picotte

from *Homeward the Arrow's Flight* by Marion Marsh Brown

Susan La Flesche Picotte was the first female Native American doctor in the United States. After completing medical school she returned to her home and began work as the doctor at the reservation school. In this excerpt, the beginning of her jobs as school doctor and as doctor for the whole reservation is told.

It was a bad winter, one of the worst Nebraska had seen in many a year. The north wind blew in icy gusts, finding its way around poorly fitted window frames and under ill-hung doors into the Omahas' houses. Many of the houses were getting old and they had not been kept in repair.

One morning when Susan started for school, the wind was particularly vicious. Reluctantly, she turned Pie, her horse, into it. When they reached the schoolgrounds, she put him immediately into the shed that was provided for bad days. As she turned to the schoolhouse, she noted that the sky looked ominous. It took all her strength to wrench the door open against the wind. "I think we're going to get snow," she called to Marguerite as she entered.

Marguerite turned back, and Susan saw the worried look on her face. "Oh dear, I hope not. Charlie's sick again. He has an awful cough, Sue, and he was so hot last night. I know he has a fever. And he went out to look after the stock this morning. I was hoping you could go by and see him this afternoon."

"Of course I'll go. A little snow won't stop me," Susan replied with a smile, hoping to cheer her sister.

As the morning progressed, the wind howled and the snow grew heavier. In a moment's lull in her work, Susan glanced out the window and discovered she could no longer see the row of trees that formed a windbreak for the school building. She felt a little tug of concern. Some of the children lived quite a distance from school. Perhaps they should be getting home.

It wasn't long until the teachers were consulting her. "Do you think we should dismiss school? If it keeps this up . . ."

"I think it would be wise to get the children on their way. It certainly isn't getting any better."

So an early dismissal was agreed upon.

Susan was helping the teachers bundle the children into coats and overshoes, tying mufflers over mouths and noses, and giving instruction to the older ones to keep a tight hold on the hands of younger brothers and sisters, when the outside door burst open and a man stumbled in. He was so caked in snow that at first she didn't recognize him.

"Dr. Susan!" he cried. "Come quick! My Minnie . . ."

"Oh, it's you, Joe," she said. "Has your wife started labor?"

He nodded. "But she's bad, Doctor. Not like before."

"Come on in and warm up, then go home and put lots of water on the stove to heat. I'll be along shortly."

Joe didn't linger. As soon as the children were on their way and she had straightened up her office, Susan sought out Marguerite. "I'll have to wait to see Charlie until after I deliver Minnie Whitefeather's baby. Joe says she's having a bad time, so I may be late."

"All right. Be sure to bundle up," Marguerite said. "It looks like the storm's getting worse."

"That I will. I always come prepared!" Susan assured her. She pulled her stocking cap down over her ears and donned the heavy wool mittens her mother had knitted for her.

"I hope you'll be all right," Marguerite said. "It's a long way over there."

"Don't worry. You can depend on Pie!" Susan waved a cheery good-bye and plunged out into the storm. She had to fight her way to the shed. Already drifts were piling high. "I hope the children are all safely home by now," she thought. Her pony was nervous. "Good old Pie," she said, patting the sleek neck as she mounted. "When you were a young one and we went racing across the hills, you didn't think you were going to have to plow through all kinds of weather with me when you grew old, did you?"

The Whitefeathers lived on the northernmost edge of the reservation. Susan turned Pie onto the road, and he plodded into the storm. "Good boy!" she said encouragingly. But she couldn't hear her words above the violent shrieking of the wind. Nor, shortly, could she tell whether they were following the road; she could only trust Pie.

It seemed to her that the storm grew worse by the minute. Suddenly Pie stopped, turning his head back as if asking Susan what he should do. She tried to wipe the caked snow from her eyes to see what was wrong and found that her fingers were stiff. But she saw Pie's problem. A huge drift lay across their path. "We'll have to go around it, Pie." She pulled him to the left until they reached a point where the drift tapered off. Pie moved around it, and Susan thought, "Now can we find the road again—if we were on the road?" She pulled on the right rein. But she couldn't tell whether they were going north, for now the storm seemed to be swirling around them from all directions.

Soon another drift blocked their way. But this time Pie wallowed through with a strange, swimming motion. How did he know he could get through that

Name _____ Date _____

one and not the other, she wondered. Suddenly, having maneuvered the drift, the pony stopped.

"Get up, Pie! We have to go on!" she urged. He did not move. She slapped the stiff reins on his neck, but to no avail. She tried kicking his sides with feet she discovered were numb. "We'll freeze to death! Go on!" Still Pie refused to move.

At length she dismounted. If she could walk on her numb feet, perhaps she could lead him. Stumbling, she made her way to Pie's head.

Then she saw, and she caught her breath in terror. For Pie stood with his head directly over a bundle in the snow—a bundle that she knew instantly was a child.

"Oh, my!" she cried. She lifted the bundle into her arms. It was a boy, one of the little ones they had turned out of school to find his way home. "What were we thinking of?" Susan railed at herself. "Jimmy! Jimmy!" she cried, shaking the child. She scooped the snow off his eyelids. He stirred, and then his eyelids lifted. "Jimmy! It's Dr. Sue. You were asleep, Jimmy. You have to wake up now." She hoisted him in front of her on the pony, and, holding him close to give him warmth from her body, she beat on his arms.

The minute she was back in the saddle, Pie moved on. "Pie! Bless you. You probably saved Jimmy's life."

As Pie pressed on, she continued to talk to Jimmy, working on him as she talked—rubbing his hands, cradling his face against her. "We have to warm up your nose," she told him. He began to cry. "You mustn't cry. Your tears will make cakes of ice!"

She strained her eyes ahead, but she could see nothing against the driving snow. She had no idea how long they had been in this frozen white nightmare. Surely if they were going in the right direction, they should have reached the Whitefeathers' by now. "Pie's going to take us to where it's nice and warm," she soothed Jimmy. And to herself she said, "If he doesn't, it's the end for all of us, you and me and him. And maybe Minnie Whitefeather and her child too."

She tried to keep Jimmy awake, finding to her consternation that she herself was growing drowsy. She well knew that to go to sleep was a sure way to freeze to death.

She must have dozed briefly, for she started when Pie suddenly stopped. She roused herself to urge him on. "Get up, Pie! We can't stop now! We have Jimmy!" She kicked his sides, but the pony refused to move. The snow had again caked her eyelids, and she pawed at it with unfeeling fists. She supposed they'd come to another drift Pie couldn't manipulate.

As she blinked hard to see, she was suddenly aware of a sound that was not born of the storm. Pie had whinnied. She even felt the ripple of his neck.

132 Lesson 6 • Unit Activity

Unit 3 • **Movement**

Name _____ Date _____

What did it mean?

Then she saw! They were by the side of a building, sheltered from the wind. It was a barn!

"Pie! Pie! You did it!" she cried.

As she tried stiffly to dismount with Jimmy, strong arms were supporting her. It was Joe.

"We are so glad you're here, Dr. Sue. We were afraid you would not make it."

"So was I," Susan said. "Please take care of Pie. We wouldn't be here except for him."

Susan delivered a baby girl that night, but she did not get to Marguerite and Charlie's. Nor did she get to her sister's home for the two days following, for the storm raged on fiercely through the night, wrapping the reservation in a tight white cocoon that could not be penetrated. There was no way to return Jimmy to his home or to let his parents know that he was safe. Susan agonized over this, but there was nothing she could do.

There were two other Whitefeather children, and Susan noticed that they came to have their hands washed before a meal. She noticed other things too: the family's clothes were clean, and so were the blankets on the beds. "You're doing well with your little family," she praised Minnie.

Minnie smiled. "Remember the summer you were home from school when you rode around trying to teach people to wash their hands before meals? We believed you—about germs and all."

"And now you're teaching your children," Susan said approvingly. "That's fine, Minnie. It means the upcoming generation will have a better time of it."

On Mars!
from *A Princess of Mars*
by Edgar Rice Burroughs (Adapted)

I opened my eyes upon a strange and weird landscape. I knew that I was on Mars. I seemed to be lying in a deep, circular basin, along the outer verge of which I could distinguish the irregularities of low hills.

Here and there were slight outcroppings of rock; and a little to my left appeared a low-walled area about four feet in height. No water and no other plants than the moss was in evidence, and as I was somewhat thirsty I determined to do a little exploring.

Springing to my feet I received my first Martian surprise, for the effort, which on Earth would have brought me standing upright, carried me into the Martian air to the height of about three yards. I alighted softly upon the ground, however. I knew that I must learn to walk all over again.

I wanted, however, to explore the low-walled area which was the only evidence of life in sight, and so I crawled. I did fairly well at this and in a few moments had reached the low wall.

There seemed to be no doors or windows upon the side nearest me, but as the wall was but about four feet high I cautiously gained my feet and peered over the top upon the strangest sight it had ever been given me to see.

The roof was of solid glass, and beneath this were several hundred large eggs, perfectly round and snowy white. The eggs were nearly uniform in size being about two and one-half feet in diameter.

Five or six had already hatched, and the ugly creatures sat blinking in the sunlight. They seemed mostly head, with little scrawny bodies, long necks and six legs, or, as I afterward learned, two legs and two arms, with a middle pair of limbs which could be used at will as either arms or legs. Their eyes were set at the sides of their heads, so this odd animal could look in any direction without turning the head.

The ears were small, cup-shaped antennae, sticking out not more than an inch. Their noses were slits in the center of their faces, in between their mouths and ears. They have lower tusks that curve upward to sharp points.

As I stood watching the ugly little monsters break from their shells I failed to notice the coming of twenty full-grown Martians behind me.

A little sound made me turn, and there, not ten feet from me, was the point of a huge spear—a spear forty feet long—tipped with gleaming metal. It was held by a man, for such I may call him, who was fully fifteen feet in height. On Earth he would have weighed some four hundred pounds. He sat on a huge animal while the hands of his two right arms held his huge spear low at the side of his mount; his two left arms were outstretched laterally to help him keep his balance.

As I had no weapons, I gave a superhuman leap to reach the top of the Martian wall. This leap carried me thirty feet into the air and landed me a hundred feet from my pursuers and on the opposite side of the walled area.

I landed on the soft moss, and, turning, saw my enemies lined up along the further wall. Some were looking at me with expressions which I afterward discovered showed extreme surprise.

They were speaking to each other in low tones and pointing toward me. I was to learn later that they were most impressed by my great jump.

The Martians, after speaking for a short time, turned and rode away in the direction from which they had come, leaving just one alone by the walled area. When they had covered perhaps two hundred yards they stopped and sat watching the warrior by the walled area.

He seemed to be the leader of the band, as I had seen that they seemed to have moved because of his orders. He dismounted, threw down his spear, and came around the end of the wall toward me unarmed.

When he was within about fifty feet of me he took off an enormous metal armband, and holding it toward me in the open palm of his hand, spoke to me in a language I could not understand. He then stopped as though waiting for my answer.

I guessed that he was saying he wanted peace. The throwing down of his weapons and the withdrawing of his troop would have meant a peaceful mission anywhere on Earth, so why not, then, on Mars!

Placing my hand over my heart I bowed low to the Martian and explained to him that while I did not understand his language, his actions spoke for the peace and friendship that were most dear to my heart. Stretching my hand toward him, I took the armband from his open palm, putting it around my arm above the elbow; I smiled at him and stood waiting.

His wide mouth spread into an answering smile, and locking one of his middle arms in mine we turned and walked back toward his mount. The fellow lifted me up behind him on the glossy back of his mount, where I hung on as best I could.

The entire group then turned and galloped away toward the range of hills in the distance.

Animal Language

from *The Story of Dr. Doolittle* by Hugh Lofting

In a small town called Puddleby-on-the-March lives a doctor named John Dolittle. The doctor is well-liked by all the people in the little town, but fewer and fewer people are coming to him when they are sick. Doctor Dolittle loves animals, and he shares his small house on the edge of town with rabbits, mice, chickens, pigeons, cows, horses, and several other pets. Two of his favorite pets are Jip, his dog, and Polynesia the parrot. Not all his patients are as fond of animals as he is. As a result, many travel to distant towns to visit other doctors when they are sick. Doctor Dolittle slowly loses all his patients but one: Cat's-meat-Man, who does not get sick very often. So what can become of a doctor who has no patients?

It happened one day that the Doctor was sitting in his kitchen talking with the Cat's-meat-Man who had come to see him with a stomach-ache.

"Why don't you give up being a people's doctor, and be an animal doctor?" asked the Cat's-meat-Man.

The parrot, Polynesia, was sitting in the window looking out at the rain and singing a sailor-song to herself. She stopped singing and started to listen.

"You see, Doctor," the Cat's-meat-Man went on, "you know all about animals—much more than what these here vets do. That book you wrote—about cats—why, it's wonderful! I can't read or write myself—or maybe I'd write some books. But my wife, Theodosia, she's a scholar, she is. And she read your book to me. Well, it's wonderful—that's all can be said—wonderful. You might have been a cat yourself. You know the way they think. And listen: you can make a lot of money doctoring animals. Be an animal-doctor."

When the Cat's-meat-Man had gone the parrot flew off the window onto the Doctor's table and said:

"That man's got sense. That's what you ought to do. Be an animal doctor. Give the silly people up—if they haven't brains enough to see you're the best doctor in the world. Take care of animals instead—THEY'll soon find it out. Be an animal-doctor."

"Oh, there are plenty of animal-doctors," said John Dolittle, putting the flower pots outside on the window-sill to get the rain.

"Yes, there ARE plenty," said Polynesia. "But none of them are any good at all. Now listen, Doctor, and I'll tell you something. Did you know that animals can talk?"

"I knew that parrots can talk," said the Doctor.

"Oh, we parrots can talk in two languages—people's language and bird language," said Polynesia proudly. "If I say, 'Polly wants a cracker,' you understand me. But hear this: *Ka-ka oi-ee, fee-fee?*"

"Good Gracious!" cried the Doctor. "What does that mean?"

"That means, 'Is the porridge hot yet?' in bird language."

"My! You don't say so!" said the Doctor. "You never talked that way to me before."

"What would have been the good?" said Polynesia, dusting some cracker-crumbs off her left wing. "You wouldn't have understood me if I had."

"Tell me some more," said the Doctor, all excited; and he rushed over to the dresser-drawer and came back with the butcher's book and a pencil. "Now don't go too fast—and I'll write it down. This is interesting—very interesting—something quite new. Give me the Birds' ABC first—slowly now."

So that was the way the Doctor came to know that animals had a language of their own and could talk to one another. And all that afternoon, while it was raining, Polynesia sat on the kitchen table giving him bird words to put down in the book.

At tea time, when the dog, Jip, came in, the parrot said to the Doctor, "See, HE'S talking to you."

"Looks to me as though he were scratching his ear," said the Doctor.

"But animals don't always speak with their mouths," said the parrot in a high voice, raising her eyebrows. "They talk with their ears, with their feet, with their tails—with everything. Sometimes they don't WANT to make a noise. Do you see now the way he's twitching up one side of his nose?"

"What's that mean?" asked the Doctor.

"That means, 'Can't you see that it has stopped raining?'" Polynesia answered. "He is asking you a question. Dogs nearly always use their noses for asking questions."

After a while, with the parrot's help, the Doctor got to learn the language of the animals so well that he could talk to them himself and understand everything they said. Then he gave up being a people's doctor altogether.

As soon as the Cat's-meat-Man had told every one that John Dolittle was going to become an animal doctor, old ladies began to bring him their pet pugs and poodles who had eaten too much cake; and farmers came many miles to show him sick cows and sheep.

One day a plow horse was brought to him; and the poor thing was terribly glad to find a man who could talk in horse language.

"You know, Doctor," said the horse,

"that vet over the hill knows nothing at all. He has been treating me six weeks now—for spavins. What I need is SPECTACLES. I am going blind in one eye. There's no reason why horses shouldn't wear glasses, the same as people. But that stupid man over the hill never even looked at my eyes. He kept on giving me big pills. I tried to tell him; but he couldn't understand a word of horse-language. What I need is spectacles."

"Of course—of course," said the Doctor. "I'll get you some at once."

"I would like a pair like yours," said the horse—"only green. They'll keep the sun out of my eyes while I'm plowing the Fifty Acre Field."

"Certainly," said the Doctor. "Green ones you shall have."

"You know, the trouble is, sir," said the plow horse as the Doctor opened the front door to let him out—"the trouble is that ANYBODY thinks he can doctor animals just because the animals don't complain. As a matter of fact it takes a much cleverer man to be a really good animal-doctor than it does to be a good people's doctor. My farmer's boy thinks he knows all about horses. I wish you could see him—he has got as much brain as a potato bug. He tried to put a mustard plaster on me last week."

"Where did he put it?" asked the Doctor.

"Oh, he didn't put it anywhere—on me," said the horse. "He only tried to. I kicked him into the duck pond."

"Well, well!" said the Doctor.

"I'm a pretty quiet creature as a rule," said the horse—"very patient with people—don't make much fuss. But I just couldn't bear it any more."

"Did you hurt the boy much?" asked the Doctor.

"Oh, no," said the horse. "I kicked him in the right place. The vet's looking after him now. When will my glasses be ready?"

"I'll have them for you next week," said the Doctor. "Come in again Tuesday—Good morning!"

Then John Dolittle got a fine, big pair of green spectacles and the plow horse stopped going blind in one eye and could see as well as ever.

And soon it became a common sight to see farm animals wearing glasses in the country round Puddleby; and a blind horse was a thing unknown.

And so, in a few years' time, every living thing for miles and miles got to know about John Dolittle, M.D. And the birds who flew to other countries in the winter told the animals in foreign lands of the wonderful doctor of Puddleby-on-the-Marsh, who could understand their talk and help them in their troubles. In this way he became famous among the animals—all over the world—better known even than he had been among the folks of the West Country. And he was happy and liked his life very much.

Answer Key

UNIT 1	UNIT 2	UNIT 3	UNIT 4	UNIT 5	UNIT 6
Quick Quiz	Quick Quiz	Quick Quiz	Quick Quiz	Quick Quiz	Quick Quiz
1. C	1. B	1. D	1. D	1. C	1. D
2. J	2. F	2. H	2. H	2. H	2. F
3. A	3. D	3. B	3. D	3. D	3. A
4. H	4. J	4. F	4. G	4. F	4. J
5. C	5. C	5. D	5. C	5. D	5. C

Spanish Vocabulary List

UNIT 1

plot trama—un grupo ordenado de eventos en una historia, libro o drama

climax clímax—el punto culminante o punto alto de la trama

resolution resolución—la parte de la trama, típicamente cerca del final, en que se resuelven los problemas o conflictos de la trama

UNIT 2

character personaje—una persona en una novela, drama o poema

motivation motivación—el motivo por el que un personaje actúa (hace algo) o habla

objective objetivo—la meta hacia la cual un personaje avanza en una escena dada; parte de la meta principal que tiene el personaje en toda la obra

UNIT 3

rhythm ritmo—en términos de movimiento, un modelo regular o irregular de movimientos

repetition repetición—en términos de movimiento, un modelo de movimientos repetidos

UNIT 4

inflection inflexión—cambios en el volumen y tono de una voz

tone tono—el uso de inflexión para comunicar emociones o ideas

UNIT 5

floor properties propiedades del piso—se llaman usualmente "props del piso," objetos encontrados en el escenario, como una lámpara o muebles

personal properties propiedades personales—usualmente llamadas, "props personales;" objetos usados por un actor

scenery la escenografía—tablas pintadas, pantallas u objetos de tres dimensiones que forman el trasfondo del escenario

UNIT 6

subject sujeto—usualmente un concepto abstracto, como miedo o poder; contesta la pregunta, "¿De qué se trata este drama?"

theme tema—la actitud hacia un sujeto comunicada a través de la acción del drama

mood talante—el sentimiento creado por una escena

Teacher's Handbook

Table of Contents

Introduction T2

Theatre Technique Tips T3

Professional Development Articles T21

Scope and Sequence of Theatre Concepts T31

Scope and Sequence of Theatre Activities T34

Glossary T35

Program Index T38

Introduction to the Teacher's Handbook

The purpose of the Teacher's Handbook is to prepare you, as the teacher, to explore and use drama in the classroom. Theatre arts, as a component of fine arts, satisfy the human need for personal expression, celebration, and communication. As students have the opportunity to tell and retell stories, create characters, and explore production elements, they will learn more about themselves and the world in which they live.

Preparing a Lesson

 ### Creating Journals

Before you begin using the theatre lessons in this book, have each student select a notebook to be used as a journal. A journal feature in each lesson provides students with an opportunity to draw or write in response to the lesson and to apply the lesson concepts to real life.

Selecting Lessons

Although all 36 lessons teach important theatre concepts, some teachers may not have the time to explore all of these lessons. Eighteen core lessons have been selected and marked with an icon in the table of contents. By using the **Unit Openers,** the core lessons, and the **Theatre Technique Tips,** it is possible to meet all of the theatre standards in the National Standards for Arts Education.

Gathering Materials

▶ In the left column of each lesson is a materials list. Before class, gather any materials needed for the lesson. These often include photocopies of a lesson **Warm-Up** page. **Read Alouds** do not need to be copied, as you will read these pages aloud to the class.

▶ The last lesson in each unit is a **Unit Activity.** The stories for these lessons are in the back of the book beginning on page 124. Sometimes these stories will need to be photocopied and distributed to students; they will not need to be copied when they are a **Read Aloud.**

Using the Theatre Technique Tips

The first section in the Teacher's Handbook is the **Theatre Technique Tips.** These tips are referenced in the lessons at point of use. Each Technique Tip covers a style of Creative Expression used in the lessons, such as pantomime or script writing. Use these tips to introduce students to the techniques the first time they are used in a lesson or for review.

Exploring the Professional Development Articles

These articles provide valuable information about the use and benefits of drama in the classroom. By covering topics such as classroom management, definitions of terms, and inclusion of students with disabilities, these articles offer the support a classroom teacher needs to implement drama in the classroom.

Using the Scope and Sequence, Glossary, and Index

The **Scope and Sequence, Glossary,** and **Index** will help you find what a concept or term means and where they are covered within this and other grade levels in *Theatre Arts Connections.*

Theatre Technique Tips

Pantomime

Focus

General Definition
Pantomime is acting without words. When actors pantomime a story they use facial expressions and expressive movements to communicate. Although there are other uses of this term, in this program *pantomime* is defined as "movement that uses silent action to tell a story."

Related Concepts
▶ Narrative pantomime, a more specific type of pantomime, involves many actors pantomiming in unison while a story or poem is read aloud. In this type of pantomime, the actors do not interact with one another; instead, all students portray characters at the same time.

▶ *Pantomime* and *mime* are not synonymous. Mime is a special art form that is closely related to pantomime; however, a mime uses a specific, stylized form of pantomime to communicate an idea and theme. Mimes often paint their faces in such a way to make their facial expressions more easily seen from a distance. Miming is an intensely disciplined art, and most mimes study specialized techniques for years.

Teach
Introduce students to skills related to pantomime in one or more of the following ways:

▶ Relaxation allows actors to use their bodies safely and expressively. Have students relax their bodies in preparation for pantomime by closing their eyes and consciously tensing and relaxing each muscle in their bodies, beginning with their toes and working their way up to their neck muscles.

▶ Discuss student observations of people's nonverbal signals in real life, such as the way slumped shoulders might communicate depression or weariness. Have students imitate some nonverbal signals, working to imagine and identify each character's specific situation, thoughts, feelings, and motivation.

▶ Discuss the importance of interacting with invisible objects in a realistic way. Have students hold two different objects, such as a pencil and a glass, noting each object's shape and weight. Have them pantomime holding one of these objects, focusing on retaining the object's exact dimensions, weight, texture, and firmness.

▶ Placement is very important in pantomime. Invisible objects such as a shelf or a door handle must remain the same throughout a pantomime. For example, if an actor pantomimes setting a glass down on a table and then returns to pick it up, the glass must appear to be in the same location in space. Have students practice this by each in turn pantomiming an interaction with an object, such as opening a door, so that the object's location does not seem to change.

Reflect
Have students consider any of the following questions that apply to their exploration of pantomime:

▶ Did your pantomime have a distinct beginning, middle, and end?

▶ Describe your character's feelings and desires. How did you use your body to communicate them?

▶ Did you use distinct body movements?

▶ How could you improve next time?

Theatre Technique Tips

Improvisation

Focus

General Definition
Improvisation is spontaneous. When students work together on improvisations, they are developing skills in creativity, imagination, and listening to others. In this program *improvisation* is defined as "acting without a script or rehearsal."

Related Concepts

▶ Scene improvisation is situation-focused. Actors may quickly choose the characters, setting, and situation (including conflict) for a scene and then act the scene out. Although it is spontaneous an improvisation of a scene should still have a beginning, a middle, and an end through which characters solve a problem.

▶ Character improvisations can allow actors to further explore characters from stories or plays. They can improvise characters interacting in situations different from those in stories, such as two actors improvising a meeting between characters from different books. Actors should focus on character details and work to infer new actions and speech based on previous characterization.

Teach
Introduce students to skills related to improvisation in one or more of the following ways:

▶ Tell students that they should usually not "deny" by contradicting other actors during an improvisation. Say, "If another actor improvises the statement, 'I love your blue hair,' do not automatically say, 'My hair isn't blue.' Accept the believability of the situation and other actors' creativity. Use your imagination to respond."

▶ Have the class improvise characters who wake up on a spaceship and must figure out how to get back to Earth.

▶ Explain that during an improvisation, actors avoid asking questions, especially questions that are answered with *yes* or *no*. These shut down the action of an improvisation. Have student pairs improvise the following: one student chooses the basic identities of two characters and their situation but keeps them secret from the other student. As they improvise the scene the student who does not know the secret facts may not ask direct questions about the facts, but must instead follow the other character's lead.

▶ Say, "Actors must focus on their characters' motivation and the conflict in the improvisation." Create an improvisation at a bus stop. Have each student decide on the facts of a certain character, including his or her motivation for being at the bus stop. Begin the improvisation, allowing students to go and wait at the bus stop as their characters and to interact with each other.

Reflect
Have students consider any of the following questions that apply to their exploration of improvisation:

▶ What were some challenges of "thinking on your feet"?

▶ Did you keep your focus on the facts of your situation and characterization? Did you work toward your character's goal?

▶ Did you accept others' ideas onstage?

Theatre Technique Tips

Theatre Games

Focus

General Definition
Theatre games are closely related to improvisation. In this program *theatre game* is defined as "an active game that helps students focus on some aspect of performance skills or story development."

Related Concepts
▶ Many theatre games focus on problem-solving skills by asking students to accomplish a goal, or focus, while observing certain rules. A student is successful during a theatre game when he or she keeps the focus and accomplishes the goal. A theatre game might involve organizing actions into a sequence of events, showing emotion through arm or leg movement alone, showing feeling using a made-up language, or group creation of a movement machine through use of repeated movements.

▶ It is often helpful to use a technique known as sidecoaching, or calling out phrases or words, to help students keep their focus on solving a problem. If students play a theatre game that is a slow-motion version of freeze tag, you might say things like, "Remember to move in slow motion! Control your bodies."

Teach
Introduce students to skills related to theatre games in one or more of the following ways:

▶ Remind students that being funny or clever is not the focus of theatre games. One type of theatre game involves creating an emotion machine. Choose an emotion, such as joy, and have one student begin repeating an action and a word or sound to illustrate joy, such as throwing his or her arms up and saying, "Hooray!" Other students should add their own repetitive actions and speech or sound to the machine, but their actions must be reactions to another student's action.

▶ Tell students that theatre games help them focus on listening to and watching each other carefully when they work together. Another theatre game is called the mirror game. Have student pairs sit across from each other. One student should act as the leader, while the other must mirror the leader's actions. They should focus on making it impossible to tell which student is the leader.

Reflect
Have students consider either of the following questions that apply to their exploration of theatre games:

▶ What was the focus of the theatre game you played? Did you keep that focus?

▶ How do you think theatre games help actors become better at playing characters?

Theatre Technique Tips

Dramatization

Focus

General Definition

Story dramatization is an important aspect of drama in the classroom. It allows students to better understand and interpret written texts by enacting the events from stories. In this program *dramatization* is defined as "using movements and dialogue to act out a scene from a story, book, play, or other text."

Related Concepts

▶ Dramatization is related to improvisation in that students are not required to memorize lines; however, dramatization differs from improvisation in that the characters, situations, and storylines are predetermined and fixed.

▶ Some story dramatizations might not involve speech; such dramatizations would be defined as pantomimes in our program, as the focus would be on physicalizing stories. Dramatizations involving dialogue without action are not categorized separately unless students are presenting a certain type of script dramatization known as Reader's Theatre.

Teach

Introduce students to skills related to dramatization in one or more of the following ways:

▶ Choose a book students have recently read as a class and a specific scene. Have students identify when and where the scene takes place, the weather, actions performed by the characters, the characters' attitudes and feelings, and any other relevant information. Have groups of students assign roles and discuss how to use speech and movement to act out this scene as the characters. For younger students, you may find it helpful to read the scene aloud, pausing at certain places to allow student groups to act out what you have just read. Discuss any choices they had to make about details that were not described in the book.

▶ Read aloud a narrative poem, such as "A Remarkable Adventure" by Jack Prelutsky. Have students listen carefully and then write or describe the events from the poem in order. Divide students into groups that contain the appropriate number of actors. Have student groups assign roles and decide how they are going to act out the characters' actions. Reread the poem, and then have student groups share their speech and actions with the class. Discuss how dramatizing the poem changed the students' understanding of the events.

Reflect

Have students consider either of the following questions that apply to their exploration of dramatization:

▶ Compare and contrast your dramatization with the book or story you dramatized. Did you change anything?

▶ How did your dramatization help you better understand the original story?

Theatre Technique Tips

Tableau

Focus

General Definition
A tableau is often used as an acting exercise, but it may also be used to begin or end a scene in a play. In this program *tableau* is defined as "a living snapshot or sculpture formed with actors' bodies that shows a moment of action in a story or illustrates the theme of a story."

Related Concepts
▶ Tableau is closely related to pantomime, as in tableaux actors must use their body positions and facial expressions to communicate characters and situations. Unlike pantomime, actors cannot use movement to further communicate. In a tableau, actors may use stylized body positions and exaggerated facial expressions.

▶ A tableau may be based on imaginary or historical characters and situations, or may illustrate character relationships from a book, play, or other existing text.

Teach
Introduce students to skills related to tableaux in one or more of the following ways:

▶ If students have not created tableaux before, you may wish to begin by having them improvise a situation or dramatize a story. Tell them to freeze, and have other students examine their body positions, describing what they know about the characters and their situations through the tableau alone. Allow student groups to plan their tableaux the second time through, choosing body positions and facial expressions that might better show their feelings and relationships.

▶ Show students the image of an appropriate photo, painting, or sculpture, and have student groups create tableaux based on this work.

▶ Have older student groups create tableaux illustrating the theme of a story or the moral of a fable. For example, students might illustrate the moral, "A friend in need is a friend indeed" by creating a tableau in which one character is helping another character study for a test. Discuss different interpretations of each theme or moral.

▶ Tell students that when creating a tableau, especially one based on a made-up situation, they need to make concrete decisions about their characters and relationships. If students do not seem to be doing this in their tableaux, hold an imaginary microphone in front of different students within a tableau, and have them speak their characters' thoughts. Take suggestions from the class as to how the bodies of the students in a tableau could show their thoughts and feelings.

Reflect
Have students consider any of the following questions that apply to their exploration of tableau:

▶ How would you compare and contrast tableaux and photographs or paintings?

▶ How did your tableau show who each character was and what his or her relationships were to the other characters?

▶ What was challenging about creating your tableau?

Theatre Technique Tips

Puppetry

Focus

Puppetry involves giving life to and creating characters from objects. In this program *puppetry* is defined as "bringing an object to life in front of an audience."

Related Concepts

▶ Shadow puppets are figures, usually two-dimensional, which are manipulated behind a screen, or stretched cloth. When a light shines on the puppets from behind the screen, they cast shadows on the screen. Sometimes actors use their hands or bodies as shadow puppets; actors may also use their bodies to create a montage, or shadow tableau.

▶ Stick puppets are cut-out shapes attached to items such as craft sticks.

▶ Hand puppets are puppets that fit over actors' hands like gloves. Sometimes they have moveable mouths; other times they may only have movable arms and heads.

▶ There are many types of puppet theatres or stages. For use in the classroom, students may create a simple stage by covering a table with a large blanket, kneeling behind it, and moving their puppets as if the top of the table is the puppets' "floor." A more complex, traditional European stage involves a three-paneled or enclosed structure. The front panel of this theatre has an opening or hole and may have curtains that open and close. Puppeteers sit within the structure and use the opening as a proscenium puppet stage. This type of puppet theatre could be simulated by cutting an opening in a trifold presentation board.

Teach

Introduce students to skills related to puppetry in one or more of the following ways:

▶ Creating puppets may involve a few simple steps or may become very complicated. To introduce students to hand puppet creation, bring in socks or mittens and allow students to glue or sew on facial features using jiggly eyes, sequins, yarn, or beads. Tell students to make a list of their characters' traits before beginning. Appropriately tailor the complexity of the materials and methods involved to the age of the students.

▶ Explain that when a hand puppet talks, its entire body should move. Other puppets onstage should freeze to indicate they are "listening." When using a moveable mouth puppet the student's fingers should move the puppet's head while his or her thumb should move the mouths. The thumb only should be moved when a puppet is speaking. Puppeteers must work to match their puppets' mouth movements to their speech. Puppets appearing from below a table stage should gradually enter while bobbing up and down as if climbing a flight of stairs; when they exit, puppets should seem to go back down a flight of stairs.

▶ Have older students create puppets with jointed arms and legs attached to rods; show examples of similar puppets from Jim Henson's Muppets or Indonesian shadow theatre.

Reflect

Have students consider either of the following questions that apply to their exploration of puppetry:

▶ What can you do as a puppeteer that you cannot do as an actor and vice versa?

▶ How could you better match your puppet's mouth movements to the words you speak?

Theatre Technique Tips

Reader's Theatre

Focus

Reader's Theatre allows students to focus on vocal characterization and sound effects. In this program *Reader's Theatre* is defined as "a style of theatre in which performers read from a script, creating characterizations through their voices, facial expressions, and upper-body posture."

Related Concepts

▶ Choral readings, in which groups or individual actors speak or chant lines, were popular in speech and drama competitions of the 1930s and 1940s. They are thought by some to be the predecessor of modern Reader's Theatre.

▶ Reader's Theatre is a presentational style of theatre; in other words the audience never forgets that what they are watching is not real life, but rather a dramatic presentation. All physical action must be imagined, as actors usually sit or stand and face the audience. Settings and costumes are limited or nonexistent.

▶ Reader's Theatre provides developing readers with an excellent opportunity to practice fluid reading. Although scripts are not memorized, always allow students time to rehearse their performances so that readers at all levels will be prepared.

Teach

Introduce students to skills related to Reader's Theatre in one or more of the following ways:

▶ Encourage students to underline or highlight the parts they read. Pauses or breaks in reading, determined through rehearsing, should be marked in some way to aid the reader. Students should decide whether they wish to use audience focus, in which all performers look at the audience while reading, offstage focus, in which performers look above the heads of the audience as if they are speaking to other, invisible characters, or (less traditionally used) onstage focus, in which performers look at one another when reading.

▶ Oral interpretation practice is important. Students need to experiment with vocal pitch, range, quality, intensity, and inflection, and learn what their voices can do. One way to do this is to present students with a simple nursery rhyme, such as "The House That Jack Built." Challenge students to say the rhyme and resist speaking in a sing-song fashion. Have them focus on the verbs and find different, appropriate ways to say them. For example, how might the verb in the line "that *kissed* the maiden all forlorn" be said differently from the verb in the line "that *killed* the rat"?

▶ Actors in Reader's Theatre often play more than one part, and doing so presents interesting challenges in vocal characterization. Have pairs of students select, adapt, or write a script containing four or more characters to perform as Reader's Theatre; challenge them to divide the roles and find ways to use their voices and facial expressions to indicate each character. They may wish to rewrite some of the descriptions of action so that they may be read by a narrator.

Reflect

Have students consider either of the following questions that apply to their exploration of Reader's Theatre:

▶ Was it challenging to act through voice and facial expressions? Why or why not?

▶ How did the Reader's Theatre performance help you better understand the reading selection?

Theatre Technique Tips

Script Writing

Focus

Writing a play allows students to directly connect skills in language arts with skills and knowledge about theatre. In this program *script writing* is defined as, "creating improvised dialogue for a monologue, short scene, or play and formalizing that dialogue by recording it or writing it in a script format."

Related Concepts

▶ Playwriting involves mastering the steps of the writing process, including inventing characters and plot situations, writing drafts, presenting readings, revising, and publishing or producing the finished work.

▶ Unlike writers of novels or short stories, a playwright's work is not fully finished until it is performed. Playwrights often revise scripts based on problems or ideas that arise during rehearsals and production.

Teach

Introduce students to skills related to script writing in one or more of the following ways:

▶ Younger students may not be able to write their own scripts. Script writing in this case should involve creating characters, improvising and refining dialogue, and recording this dialogue using audio or video recording. After reviewing their recorded dialogue, have students discuss whether their dialogue told a story with action and a beginning, a middle, and an end. Was their dialogue appropriate? Allow students to revise and replay their scripts.

▶ Encourage students to write character sketches, story ideas, and interesting verbal phrases or overheard dialogue in notebooks or journals. These ideas can be very useful when working on a script in which they are creating new and imagined characters.

▶ Encourage students working on script ideas to decide on a through line, or major action of the play, and conflict early on. What will be their story's Major Dramatic Question? What is its five *W*s? Who are the protagonist and antagonist(s)? Improvising scenes as invented characters can help students develop both character and plot ideas.

▶ Remind students that character dialogue should fit the characters. Their words and phrasing should match their personalities, times in which they live, social and economic situations, and emotional state. Students should also consider how easily their scripts can be staged.

▶ Have students use traditional script formatting. Characters should be introduced in a list form at the beginning of the script. When a character speaks in the play, his or her name should be set to the left of the line and be followed by a colon or period. Stage directions and descriptions of a character's attitude when speaking should be set in parentheses and italics (or should be written in a different color of ink if handwritten).

Reflect

Have students consider any of the following questions that apply to their exploration of script writing:

▶ Did your scene, monologue, or play have a clear beginning, middle, and end?

▶ Who was your protagonist or main character? What did he or she want to achieve? What obstacles made this goal difficult to pursue?

▶ How would you like to stage your play? Who would you cast as your characters?

Theatre Technique Tips

Storytelling

Focus

Storytelling is one of the most ancient theatrical art forms. In our program *storytelling* is defined as "the art of sharing stories with other people."

Related Concepts

▶ Throughout history, storytellers have served an important purpose. In preliterate cultures a storyteller was the keeper of a culture's history, beliefs, and traditions. Stories had to be passed from one generation to another, and thus traditional stories were often structured in a way that made them easier to remember, such as creating groups of three characters or events or repeating certain phrases over and over within a story.

▶ Storytelling in America has experienced a revival in the last hundred years. In the early twentieth century, American libraries first began to offer story hours for children. A few professional storytellers from England and Europe came and taught storytelling techniques to librarians, teachers, and many other interested people. In 1903 Richard T. Wyche organized the National Story League at the University of Tennessee, which began a revival of the art of storytelling in the South. Today there are many ways to experience American storytellers through live or recorded performances.

Teach

Introduce students to skills related to storytelling in one or more of the following ways:

▶ Storytelling is closely related to acting. A storyteller should use vocal and facial expressions to create characters and engage an audience. Give students time to practice telling stories they plan to share with others, working in groups to give each other constructive feedback to help improve each story. Storytellers should focus on making eye contact with the audience. They should focus on the audience's responses, slowing down, speeding up, and emphasizing parts of their stories so that the audience fully engages with and understands a story.

▶ Stories explaining how something in nature came to be are told throughout the world. Have students select a phenomenon or object in nature, such as the rainbow or the sun. Allow them to make up stories explaining its beginning, such as where the first rainbow came from or why the sun seems to cross the sky.

▶ Students may find it helpful to create outlines of stories they plan to tell. They do not need to memorize stories, but they should have a clear understanding of the order of events.

▶ Storytelling in the classroom can provide students with a way to share personal stories or stories from their heritages. Have students share such stories.

▶ There are many interesting storytelling traditions from other cultures, such as the "call-and-response" tradition in some parts of Africa. Have students research different storytelling traditions from cultures around the world and restructure a familiar story to match each of these styles.

Reflect

Have students consider either of the following questions that apply to their exploration of storytelling:

▶ How did you change your voice when you spoke as different characters? Were you able to keep each characterization consistent?

▶ What memory techniques could you use to help you remember the sequence of events in a story?

Theatre Technique Tips

Creative Movement

Focus

In this program *creative movement* is defined as "nonrealistic, expressive movement that allows a performer to communicate a concept or idea, such as joy or struggle, or to become a natural force or object, such as the wind."

Related Concepts

▶ *Creative movement* is a term constructed to cover a variety of movement styles that involve elements of dance. Rather than being realistic character movement, creative movement allows students to express themselves through improvised, free-form movement.

▶ Exploration of movement is an important tool for actors. It can be used as a valuable warm-up to get creative ideas flowing, and it can help actors overcome their inhibitions.

Teach

Introduce students to skills related to creative movement in one or more of the following ways:

▶ Choose pairs of contrasting ideas or emotions, such as freedom and bondage or terror and peace. Have students move around the room in a way that expresses one of these ideas; for example, they could stretch out their arms and then contract their bodies while looking around to show terror. When you use a signal such as a sound or word, they should change their movements to express the contrasting idea. Discuss the different types of movement that best showed each concept.

▶ Creative movement can be useful as a warm-up when portraying unusual fantasy characters. Have students choose a fairy tale or myth in which natural forces are personified, such as "The Rat Bride" from Japan. As a class, explore different creative movements that could show the force of the wind or the movement of waves. Work to incorporate these movements into actors' performances as these characters.

▶ Have students attempt to show an idea or emotion using controlled, repetitive movement of isolated body parts, such as their arms or feet alone.

▶ Discuss plays or performances in which abstract movement could be used. For older students, connect creative movement with presentational theatre, or theatre in which actors do not seek to emulate real life but rather are clearly presenting a performance.

Reflect

Have students consider either of the following questions that apply to their exploration of creative movement:

▶ How did using creative movement affect the way you felt while performing?

▶ What types of movements did you use? How did you use isolated body parts? How did you use rhythm and repetition?

Theatre Technique Tips

Dramatic Movement

Focus

When students use dramatic movement they practice showing characters through their posture and movement. In this program *dramatic movement* is defined as "a characterization exercise in which the focus is on revealing character through movement."

Related Concepts

▶ In the context of acting, dramatic movement can be very useful in building a character. Actors often use movement exercises, such as moving as their characters performing everyday tasks like getting dressed, to explore particular characters and to help them make choices about the way they will move onstage.

▶ Dramatic movement differs from pantomime in that it is not concerned with plot or conflict, but instead focuses wholly on physical characterization.

Teach

Introduce students to skills related to dramatic movement in one or more of the following ways:

▶ Choose a time period students have been studying in social studies. Discuss the types of dress worn by people in that time and culture, how people may have related to one another, and daily activities they probably performed. Have students use prop or costume pieces to help them understand the way people in that time would have moved; for example, they could simulate bustles by tying pillows onto themselves. Have students each select one character from this time period and act as this character getting dressed or preparing a meal.

▶ Have students all move as the same character performing a simple task, such as setting the table for supper. Call out different characters, such as a ballet dancer, a baby, or a penguin, and have students show the way each character might perform the activity.

▶ Have students choose animal characters. Assign each student a different emotion, and then have students move as their animal characters would move when affected by each emotion.

Reflect

Have students consider any of the following questions that apply to their exploration of dramatic movement:

▶ How did you hold your body when acting as your character? Compare and contrast this movement style with the way you usually move in real life.

▶ How did motivation and emotion influence the way you moved as your character?

▶ How did you keep your characterization consistent? Was it challenging to do so? Why or why not?

Theatre Technique Tips

Sound Effects

Focus

Creating and using sound effects in a theatrical performance is an important element of production. In this program *sound effects* are defined as "sounds and music created and used onstage to motivate action, communicate setting, or create mood."

Related Concepts

▶ Sound effects are an essential element of production. Sound effects used in live theatre may be live, or created at the time they are needed, or recorded prior to the performance. Mechanical sound effects help motivate action onstage. Environmental sound effects help create setting and mood; in radio drama these types of sound effects are vital to creating an image in the mind of the listener.

▶ Music in a performance can serve many of the same functions as sound effects. Music is sometimes a part of a scene's setting, as in the music played during a scene set at a ball. Transitional music plays between scenes and helps maintain the play's mood. Incidental music is another type of music used in plays; it is played in the background of a scene and also helps to create mood.

▶ Sound effects can be created using many common items. Crinkling cellophane paper can create the sound of a fire burning. Students can "walk" heavy boots across two layered boards or a box filled with gravel to create footsteps. Teacups and saucers can create the sound of rattling dishes. Large metal spoons clinked together sound like swords in a duel. A synthesizer can be used to create many interesting sound effects.

Teach

Introduce students to skills related to sound effects in one or more of the following ways:

▶ Have students watch a scene from a video and then make a list of all the sound effects. Replay the scene, and compare it with students' lists. Alternatively, have students watch a scene from a video with sound muted, and have them predict the effects used.

▶ Have students bring in recordings of their favorite music; select several of these and discuss the types of feelings each song evokes. Have groups of students improvise scenes that reflect each mood.

▶ Read aloud or discuss a story that takes place in a specific location, such as "Hansel and Gretel," which takes place in a forest, or bring in a book of age-appropriate scripts for older students to analyze. Discuss different possible sound effects, such as sounds that evoke setting (crickets chirping, city sounds) and sounds that motivate action onstage (a doorbell ringing, a car horn honking). If you wish, have groups of students create and record several of the necessary sound effects.

Reflect

Have students consider either of the following questions that apply to their exploration of sound effects:

▶ How does music affect your mood? How did you use music or how could you use music to create mood in a drama?

▶ Which sound effects were most effective? What are some of the challenges of creating and using sound effects for live theatre?

Theatre Technique Tips

Sensory Recall

Focus

Sensory recall or sense memory is a tool many actors use in the process of characterization. In this program *sensory recall* is defined as, "the use of remembered sights, sounds, smells, tastes, and textures to define character."

Related Concepts

▶ Sensory recall can be very useful to actors onstage. If an actor is supposed to act as though a cup of water is actually a cup of hot tea, he or she can use memories of the sensation of drinking a hot beverage to help create realistic reactions onstage.

▶ Characters' reactions to sensory stimuli can also communicate information about who they are or how they are feeling. When actors use sensory recall, they use their imaginations to transport themselves as their characters into particular situations, taking into account the characters' ages and physical, social, and emotional states.

▶ To use sensory recall, it is easiest to think about the small details of a memory. For example, instead of trying to remember how it feels to be hot by thinking about "hotness," remember how sweat feels as it trickles down the back of your neck or the sticky feeling of a sweaty shirt clinging to you. As an actor, using this memory and then physicalizing actions that one would take in response to it—for example, pulling at the clinging shirt or wiping the sweat off of your neck—will help recreate the sensation.

Teach

Introduce students to skills related to sensory recall in one or more of the following ways:

▶ Discuss with students the importance of imagination when acting. Pass around concrete objects, such as a coin, a brittle leaf, and a heavy book. Then have students pretend to pass around these same objects. Encourage them to use their memories of their previous interactions with these objects to help them imagine them.

▶ Have students choose a particular character and scene from a book they recently read as a class. Discuss physical sensations the character experiences in that scene. Have students identify experiences of similar sensations they have had, and have all students simultaneously move as that character, using those remembered sensations to help them act as the character.

▶ Discuss ways in which students could use details of sense memories they have when playing a character in a fantastic or unusual situation, such as a character who is experiencing life on another planet. How could they identify with that character's physical experience?

Reflect

Have students consider either of the following questions that apply to their exploration of sensory recall:

▶ How vivid or concrete was your memory of smells, tastes, and other physical sensations? Was it difficult to transfer the memory to the character's experience? Why or why not?

▶ How could you use sensory recall to help you better create a character who seems realistic?

Theatre Technique Tips

Emotional Recall

Focus

Emotional recall is another tool many actors use in the process of creating a character. In this program *emotional recall* is defined as "the technique of using emotional memories in the process of characterization."

Related Concepts

▶ Emotional recall is closely associated with a type of acting known as "the Method." The Method involves acting techniques advocated by Constantin Stanislavsky, one of the cofounders of the Moscow Art Theatre in 1898. Stanislavsky rejected acting methods of his day that seemed stilted and unnatural and wrote three famous books describing what he considered to be a more naturalistic approach to acting.

▶ Actors use emotional recall to help them enter the lives of the characters. If an actor cannot identify with a character's emotions in the given circumstances, he or she can find a memory that evokes that emotion. For example, if you cannot imagine the feeling of terror of a character in unusual danger but hate going to the dentist, you might use the memory of sitting in the waiting room of a dentist's office to identify with the character. Emotional and sensory recall are related, as specific physical details of a memory often help create that feeling. The feeling should then be applied to the characterization; actors do not think about their own memories in performances but rather make their experiences synonymous with the characters' experiences while in rehearsals.

Teach

Introduce students to skills related to emotional recall in one or more of the following ways:

▶ Discuss the ways students' memories of situations evoke emotions for them. How do specific details of those memories, such as sounds or smells they remember, make each memory seem more real?

▶ Have students close their eyes and recall a common event, such as arriving at school on the first day. Ask questions to help them remember details of that event, such as, "What was the weather like that morning? What clothes were you wearing?" and so on. After a few minutes, have students open their eyes and write journal entries describing any emotions the exercise evoked and what remembered details seemed to evoke the emotions. Explain that actors often use such details to help them experience and understand a character's feelings in a play.

▶ Have students choose an emotionally charged scene from a story or book. Discuss the way each character is probably feeling, using evidence from the text. Have students consider what memories from their own lives might help them empathize with each character's emotions.

Reflect

Have students consider any of the following questions that apply to their exploration of emotional recall:

▶ What remembered details most strongly evoked an emotion?

▶ Why do you think the concrete details of a memory help recreate feelings you had long ago?

▶ In what various character situations could you use this specific memory?

Theatre Technique Tips

Settings

Focus

Settings in live theatre are created visually through a combination of scenery, props, and lighting. In this program *setting* is defined as "the visual elements that combine to show when and where a play takes place and to evoke mood."

Related Concepts

▶ In professional theatre, setting is created visually through a set and lighting. Students have an opportunity to experience some of the elements of theatrical production when they create or design settings or sets for dramas. In a classroom environment, settings do not need to be very complex; the important thing is for students to consider the time and location in which a play takes place and utilize available resources to suggest that time and location. For example, students can drape blankets over chairs or desks to create scenery that evokes mountains or waves. Students might paint or draw a scenic backdrop, hang it, and then dramatize or improvise a scene in front of it.

▶ Although props are a part of the creation of setting, the use of props is covered separately on page T20.

Teach

Introduce students to skills related to settings in one or more of the following ways:

▶ Have students each make a list of every visual detail they can remember that is related to a familiar setting. Discuss their lists. What elements would be essential when communicating that location to an audience? What elements would not be necessary? Discuss choices that set designers must make when creating limited or streamlined sets.

▶ Sets are not always realistic. Sometimes scenery or props may be used symbolically to show a central theme of a production or to create mood. Older students may enjoy the challenge of creating set designs that show the theme or mood of a familiar book. You might also challenge them to create an abstract, symbolic setting for a play version of a favorite film.

▶ Discuss how details of setting affect characters in a scene. How can actors show setting through movement alone? Have students move as a character from a story with which they are familiar. Call out changes to the character's setting and have students adjust their movements. For example, if the story takes place in a desert, change the setting to a ship at sea and have students adjust their movements.

Reflect

Have students consider any of the following questions that apply to their exploration of settings:

▶ How did you create setting through your design, set creation, or movement?

▶ If you created scenery, how did it help show time, place, mood, and/or theme?

▶ Do you think sets are an essential element of theatre? Why or why not?

Theatre Technique Tips

Costumes

Focus

Costumes are an important part of play production. They help show who a character is and when and where a play takes place, and they are part of the overall visual design of a play. In this program *costumes* are defined as "the clothing and accessories worn by actors in a drama."

Related Concepts

▶ For students to fully explore the details of theatre it is important that they begin to identify and experiment with the role of clothing in characterization. In professional theatre other factors beyond characterization must be considered when costumes are designed. The costumes must both reveal characters and relate visually to the overall design and tone of a production.

▶ In classroom drama students should begin by experimenting with simple costume pieces, such as hats or scarves. For simplicity's sake, students can create costume pieces using materials such as paper grocery bags or posterboard. Make sure that all available materials are age-appropriate, and help younger students by performing tasks such as stapling or cutting through thick board.

▶ Although makeup and masks are a part of costume, their use is covered separately on page T19.

Teach

Introduce students to skills related to costumes in one or more of the following ways:

▶ Have students each choose one character from a book with which they are familiar. Tell them to imagine they must reveal this character through one costume piece only. What would be essential for that character? Have students each describe the costume piece and explain why it best shows who that character is.

▶ Have students attend a live amateur or professional theatre performance; alternatively, have them view a recording of such a performance. Discuss the ways in which costumes related to the style and color of the scenery and props. How did they help reveal who each character was?

▶ Have older students do further research on clothing related to a culture or time period they are learning about in their social studies curriculum. You may wish to have them do image searches using an Internet search engine as well as use printed resources such as encyclopedias and other books. Have each student use his or her research to create a costume design for a character from that time period. Discuss choices a costume designer might make that could depart from strict authenticity and why he or she might make such choices.

Reflect

Have students consider any of the following questions that apply to their exploration of costumes:

▶ How did the five *W*s of the story relate to your design of costumes? How did your costume reflect the character and setting?

▶ How did you use color in your costume?

▶ What types of considerations must a costume designer make when he or she is designing costumes? Why do you think he or she ought to work with the set and lighting designers?

Theatre Technique Tips

Makeup and Masks

Focus

Makeup and masks help reveal who characters are. Makeup may merely accentuate an actor's features. It can be realistic or fantastic. In this program *makeup* and *masks* are defined as "elements used to highlight or alter an actor's face."

Related Concepts

▶ Masks have been used in cultures around the world. Often performers have used masks for ceremonial purposes, seeking to become, embody, or personify another person or deity. Masks change a performer's face in a drastic way—for this reason, students who are reluctant to participate in dramatic activities may find mask work freeing, as masks can allow them to perform while feeling "hidden."

▶ Actors in professional, live theatre often design and apply their own makeup. Makeup skills are therefore essential for actors who perform in plays. Although students may learn a few of these skills, students in younger grades should feel free to experiment with makeup elements without focusing on complex, technical skills.

Teach

Introduce students to skills related to makeup and masks in one or more of the following ways:

▶ For the purposes of safety, do not allow students to apply makeup on each other. Make sure that each student uses his or her own brush, sponge, or cotton ball to apply his or her makeup, and that each student has access to a mirror. Emphasize the importance of safety when using makeup near eyes, noses, or mouths, and always be sure to keep the activity on-level and age appropriate.

▶ Allow younger students to create masks and then use face paint to transform their faces into those of animal or fantasy creatures. Compare and contrast the way masks and makeup change their faces. Which do students prefer for certain characters, and why?

▶ For older students who have studied principles of visual art, it may be helpful to note that realistic makeup application involves techniques that are similar to those of a portrait artist. Highlights, shading, and color value are all important in makeup application. If possible provide students with cream foundations of various shades and makeup sponges (one per student). Have students choose foundations that blend well with their skin colors and apply a thin coat of the foundations to their faces using the sponges. Explain that this acts as a blank canvas. Have them experiment with application of lighter and darker foundations to accentuate their facial features.

Reflect

Have students consider either of the following questions that apply to their exploration of makeup and masks:

▶ Describe the makeup or mask you created or designed. How did your mask or makeup show who the character is?

▶ Compare and contrast the challenges associated with the use of makeup and masks. In what situations would one be more effective than the other?

Theatre Technique Tips

Props

Focus

Properties, commonly referred to as *props*, are an essential component of a play's setting. In this program *props* are defined as "objects found or used onstage, including furniture and items used and carried by actors."

Related Concepts

▶ There are three main types of props: floor props, personal or hand props, and decorative props. Floor props are often items such as furniture, lamps, or tables. Personal props are objects carried and used by actors; they are often small objects, such as pens or money. Decorative props are props that help reveal setting, such as a portrait or painting on a wall.

▶ Like sound effects, props can serve a variety of aesthetic and functional purposes. They can help show who characters are and when and where a play takes place. They can motivate or be an integral part of a plot. They can help create mood and show a play's theme.

▶ In classroom drama props can be simple. Use objects from the classroom whenever possible or allow students to bring in objects from home. Allow students to imaginatively pretend one object is actually another; for example, a pen could be used as a microscope or as a microphone. Have students create props using art supplies such as clay, masking tape, or posterboard.

Teach

Introduce students to skills related to props in one or more of the following ways:

▶ Explain to students that stage business, which involves the use of props and parts of the set, is an essential part of acting. Actors must seem comfortable and at ease as they interact with props onstage. The correct and safe use of certain historical props, such as swords or fans, may require special training. Have volunteers act as a character writing a letter to a friend. Discuss details of such an action and how the character might interact with props such as a pen, a desk, and sheets of paper. How would the time period affect the character's actions and the props he or she would use?

▶ Explain to students that technical rehearsals are an important part of theatrical productions. They allow the technical crew to practice performing all the technical tasks related to a production, including setting (or placing) and striking (or removing) the props. When students work with props in dramatic activities, have them practice setting and striking the props in an orderly manner. If possible have some students act as the stage crew while others work as the actors. Discuss the importance of speed and consistency when placing, moving, and removing props.

Reflect

Have students consider any of the following questions that apply to their exploration of props:

▶ How do props affect the way actors move onstage? How have they affected your own performances?

▶ What was challenging about setting and striking props?

▶ How can props create both setting and mood?

Professional Development

Planning and Managing Drama Activities

by Betty Jane Wagner
Roosevelt University

Because drama can overexcite students, it is important to establish rules and signals carefully in advance. Ideally, the students and the teacher should do this together, as planning and evaluating the effectiveness of a drama afterward are crucial parts of the whole process. You will need to freeze the action from time to time to keep the drama from spinning out of control or into silliness. You can use a bell, a couple of sharp raps on a tambourine, a loud clap, or a verbal signal, such as, "Freeze." Practice responding to the signal a few times until everyone understands.

One problem that often arises in an improvisational drama is giggling. When students are shy and embarrassed, they tend to laugh instead of staying in role and playing their parts with belief and seriousness. Talk about this ahead of time. Remind the students that when they giggle and step out of role, they make it very hard for the other students to stay focused. Tell them you will stop the drama when they find it to hard to stay serious. If only one child "loses it," go over to him or her and say, "I know this is hard for you. Please take your seat until you feel you can join us without giggling." Stop the drama entirely whenever a few students do not appear to be "with it."

Take time to establish roles before the drama begins. You might start by having everyone in the class stand as if they are, for example, an elderly woman with not enough to eat. Have all the students simultaneously pantomime the posture and facial expression of that character.

Starting with pantomime is probably the easiest way to introduce dramatic activities, especially with an unruly class. You can even do this while having the students stand beside their desks. Your goal, however, should be to arrange the room—pushing aside desks or tables as needed—so that at least half of the class can work in small groups in improvising the movements of a drama.

Remember, it is not usually important that students have an audience in educational drama. The goal is to have the *experience* of role-playing, not of evoking a response in an audience. Thus, simultaneously acting out the part of each of the characters in turn while a story is being read aloud is a good way to help students focus on each of the characters before they work in small groups to assign roles and each play a different character.

Drama Terminology

by Betty Jane Wagner
Roosevelt University

The drama activities presented in this curriculum encompass both informal drama in the classroom and the more formal theatre performance for an audience. The purpose of informal drama is to enlarge and deepen vision and understanding for the *participants*. The purpose of theatre, on the other hand, is to present an enactment of human experience in order to enlighten and entertain an audience.

When a teacher conducts an informal drama, it may be termed either *creative drama, educational drama* (or *drama in education*), or, more recently, *process drama*. The goal of all of these is an educational one: to help students come to understand human interactions, empathize with other persons, and internalize alternate points of view. There is no emphasis on training actors for the stage. Brian Way describes the goal of this type of drama as leading "the inquirer to moments of direct experience, transcending mere knowledge, enriching the imagination, possibly touching the heart and soul as well as the mind" (Development Through Drama, New York: Humanities, 1972, p. 1).

Creative drama is the older term for informal classroom drama. The action in creative drama is often suggested by a story, poem, original idea, or music provided by a child or adult. Both creative drama and educational drama may include pantomime. Both are developed through improvisation and role-playing, but educational drama is less likely than creative drama to have a beginning, a middle, and an end and to begin with a warm-up and end with relaxation exercises.

In educational or process drama, as in creative drama, the action may be introduced with a story. More commonly, however, the students are asked to confront a situation lifted from history or contemporary life. When a problem or conflict is introduced from an area of the curriculum, the students are expected to respond in role, usually as persons of authority. There is less emphasis on story and character development and more emphasis on problem solving or living through a particular moment in time. Through ritual, dramatic encounters, pantomime, writing in role, reflection, and tableaux, students enter the lives of imagined characters and play out their responses to challenges and crises. Experienced educational-drama teachers often initiate the drama or move this along by assuming a role themselves; in role, they can heighten tension by challenging the participants to respond in believable ways.

Unlike creative and educational drama, whose focus is process, the focus in theatre is on *product*—a finished, polished production for an audience. Whenever students work together to prepare a drama for an audience, they are engaging in theatre. Theatre experiences build confidence and awareness of the power of theatre elements such as movement versus inaction, sound versus silence, and light versus darkness. Students who are rehearsing in preparation for a theatre performance need to be aware of the need to project their voices so all can hear, to keep their bodies facing the invisible "fourth wall," and to use gestures and actions more deliberately in order to communicate with the audience. In theatre performance the students, as actors, must accommodate for the audience and calculate the effects of their actions on that group.

Both informal drama and formal theatre have their place in the activities of the classroom. Both share the excitement and challenge of working imaginatively in role to construct contexts, events, and interactions, and both allow participants to expand their understanding of real life and the content of the curriculum.

Developmental Stages in Educational Drama

by Betty Jane Wagner
Roosevelt University

Students who are challenged or struggling readers often shine in drama activities. Often the confidence they build in drama carries over to their approach to other school tasks. Drama teachers who meet with children only for drama sessions are often surprised to find that some of the leaders in drama work are actually having difficulty in their regular academic program. Classroom teachers report that after experiencing success in drama, students improve in other areas.

It is ironic to talk about development from a more primitive to a more advanced stage of dramatic activity given the fact that drama theorists agree that preschool and primary students are the most spontaneous and uninhibited in dramatic improvisations. As they get older, students tend to lose their belief in their roles and feel self-conscious, especially if the teacher focuses too much on performance.

In R. W. Colby's 1988 groundbreaking longitudinal study of growth of dramatic intelligence, he described developmental growth as a U-shaped trajectory. His theory is that successive reorganizations of understanding account for, for example, growth from the preschool stage of *being* a character to the middle childhood stage of *playing* a character, and from that to the adolescent stage of a return to the "notion of *being* a character, but on a higher level and with the discoveries of the previous stages available" (183). In other words, both young children and teenagers can share with accomplished actors the capacity to identify with and believe that they are the characters they are performing, but in between these stages, students resort to learning from the outside rather than from the inside of the character. It is as if they perceive acting as a "game with rules," and they are trying to figure out just what the rules are. Colby characterizes this middle-childhood stage as that of *playing* a character, or pretending to be that character and glomming onto themselves whatever attributes they think their role demands. At this stage they get better at refining their register and diction for their parts, and they learn how to create gestures and actions that an audience can respond to. In the process they often lose the spontaneity that characterizes younger children.

Cognitive psychologists in their study of the spontaneous play of early childhood have found that the proportion of time spent in symbolic pretend play declines as children grow. Of all the types of play young children engage in, symbolic play decreases as games with rules increase. Jean Piaget claimed that functional (exercise or practice) play occurs during the sensorimotor stage from birth to two years. Symbolic pretend play then takes over and reaches its height between two or three and five or six years of age. By the time a child is seven or eight, games with rules that are socially transmitted become the dominant play or ludic activity, along with constructive play. Piaget's theory could account for the change in children's involvement with drama. If by seven or eight, children then treat drama as a "game with rules," they are looking for ways to learn how to *do* drama rather than simply immersing themselves *in* a role. Only later do they return to the engaged emotional identification with a character, and by then they have internalized what they have learned at the bottom part of their U-shaped trajectories.

Howard Gardner, famous for his theory of multiple intelligences, sees growth in dramatic intelligence as critical in the development of interpersonal intelligence, an art that is in much demand in our fractured and stressful society. Students who develop diverse potentials can contribute uniquely to democratic life and appreciate the differing gifts of others. No other activity teachers can foster in the classroom contributes any more to this goal than improvisational drama.

How to Respond to Classroom Drama

by Betty Jane Wagner
Roosevelt University

Do

▶ Ask the children to explore a story by acting it out together.

▶ Respond to students in role in their drama.

▶ Stop the drama whenever a group of students is acting silly, and ask them if they want to continue; if so, be sure the problem doesn't recur.

▶ After a noisy and exciting session, have the students lie on the floor as if in their beds, and reflect on how they felt and what they thought as their characters.

▶ Think of ways for students in role to write diary entries, letters, or news articles for the press.

▶ Enter the drama yourself in role as a person who heightens the tension by introducing a problem.

▶ After a drama is over, congratulate the whole group for staying in role and helping the drama along.

▶ Talk about a drama after it is over, reflecting on whether or not persons in real situations would act the way they had.

▶ Create dramas that bring literature or other curricular areas alive.

▶ Give students opportunities to depict dramatic action through drawing, dancing, or writing.

▶ Reflect as a class on the drama after the lesson is over and talk about what did and didn't work.

Don't

▶ Imply that the goal of the drama is to perform for an audience.

▶ Give directions to the group in your usual teacher stance.

▶ Ignore the behavior of a group of students who are having trouble believing their roles and are therefore giggling, rolling their eyes, or acting foolish.

▶ Keep a high-action drama going so long that the students stop thinking about their roles and instead get into heightening the conflict and "hamming it up."

▶ Separate drama from other areas of the curriculum, such as writing or reading.

▶ Let the drama lose focus by letting it continue without dramatic tension and therefore become boring.

▶ Stop the drama to congratulate a particular student, thereby creating competition rather than encouraging teamwork.

▶ Tell students what to do and how to do it before they act out a story, thus confusing them with too many directives.

▶ Set up dramas that have no relation to what students are reading in other classes.

▶ See dramatization as the end point of exploring a piece of literature or curricular area.

▶ Grade participation in a way that singles out good performers and thus sets up competition among students.

Research That Supports Educational Drama

by Betty Jane Wagner
Roosevelt University

A solid body of research shows that informal educational drama, as presented in this curriculum, is effective in improving students' oral language, reading, and writing proficiency. For a summary of the results of studies of the effects of educational drama on language arts, see <u>Educational Drama and Language Arts: What Research Shows</u> (cited on page T30).

Research indicates that participation in drama leads to improved listening, comprehension, understanding of sequence, and internalization of the grammar of a story. Moreover, when students role-play in a social studies, science, or math lesson, they comprehend the subject matter better. When students are just on the edge of understanding a topic, the pressure to talk in role as if they know it will help in the forging of meaning. Because students usually feel compelled to respond in a dramatic situation, they bring to bear all they know about a person in his or her imagined shoes and often connect their recent new knowledge with their previous experience, and in the process construct new perceptions. Once they have expressed their new understanding orally, they are more prepared to write about a topic. As students assume a variety of roles in educational drama, they develop a wider range of strategies for dealing with conflicts and understanding others in the real world.

When young children play dramatically, they put themselves under pressure to use language in a more flexible and mature way. They learn very early to differentiate their voice register when talking with an imagined baby, younger child, or person in authority. In teacher-led dramas, the teacher can introduce into the drama precise vocabulary that may be unfamiliar, and the students pick up the words naturally. For example, in a drama about a hospital, young children will need to use words or phrases such as *stethoscope, urine analysis, blood test,* or *CAT scan*—all of which the teacher can supply naturally in the context of the drama. They not only expand the range of their voice register and vocabulary, but they also acquire standard dialect in an effortless way. In the process they are laying down a foundation for the acquisition of literacy because both drama and reading are symbolic acts.

Because drama is a social art, students learn that unless they cooperate and support others, the game is over. Drama also prepares children for symbolic thought. In an informal drama, real objects have to be imagined and seen in the minds of all the participants in the same way—for example, the imagined table has to be in the same spot for all of the players. In other words, the role players need to be engaging in symbolic behavior if the drama is going to work. Since all of literacy is symbolic, drama is a valuable activity to facilitate reading and writing.

Thus, although students may enjoy drama very much, it is more than fun and games. By working hard at improvisation students gain insight into the social world that surrounds them and improve their comprehension at the same time.

Theatre Arts and Students with Disabilities

by Mandy Yeager
Art Educator, Ph.D. Student
The University of North Texas at Denton

Teacher Attitudes Towards Inclusion

Any discussion of the benefits of theatre arts for students with disabilities must begin with considering teacher attitudes regarding disability and inclusion. With over six percent of all school-aged children in the United States experiencing some type of disability (United States Census, 2000), the likelihood is that students with disabilities are present in every classroom. As a result, disability becomes one of the many perspectives and voices represented in classrooms. The teacher who pays heed to diverse voices and perspectives will choose instructional methods and materials that align with the abilities and experiences of all of his or her students.

Benefits of Inclusive Theatre Arts Experiences

Students with and without disabilities have much to gain from inclusive theatre arts experiences. Research studies of students with disabilities participating in theatre arts programs report a demonstrated relationship between dramatic activities and increased academic and social skills such as oral language, on-task and courteous behavior, and conflict resolution. Positive changes in student attitudes and feelings about learning and self are most pronounced for students with disabilities.

The inclusion of students with disabilities in theatre arts programs also serves to remind teachers and nondisabled students that disability is a normal experience. Numerous studies have been conducted that prove that personal interactions with persons who are disabled are the most effective way to dispel stereotypes about disability and build equitable relationships with persons who are disabled. A curriculum and a classroom that does not ignore disability, but rather honors and addresses it, is one that prepares students for social responsibility and equity.

Practical Strategies for Inclusion

Successful adaptations for students with disabilities begin with proper attitudes towards inclusion. These attitudes should be accompanied by a willingness to obtain information about students' abilities. The Internet offers a number of resources for understanding students with disabilities. Each student with an identified disability also has an Individualized Education Plan (IEP) that details information about student learning styles, strengths, needs, and goals. The Individuals with Disabilities Education Act (IDEA) guarantees all educators of students with disabilities the right to view and receive help in implementing this plan. Other useful information about students with disabilities can be gathered through collaboration with special educators and related service personnel at the school level. These individuals can give art educators useful insight regarding successful instructional strategies and modifications for students with disabilities.

Accommodations for students with disabilities should be made in the physical space of the classroom or stage, making sure that students with mobility impairments have access to class activities. Use the principles of differentiated instruction to present material in such a way that students with cognitive disabilities can readily comprehend and apply knowledge. Provide all students opportunities to think about issues of disability through thoughtful selections of scripts and classroom activities.

Conclusion

Theatre arts have a powerful role in the education of all students, especially students with disabilities. A carefully designed program will address multiple learning and social needs of students, as well as provide them with an empowering experience.

Tips for Putting on a Class Play

✔ **Choosing a Play Script** Consider the audience and the occasion. Check for royalty fees and permission requirements. Choose plays with minimal lighting and sound. Make sure the plays require a simple set.

✔ **Young Students** It can be effective to develop a play through creative drama with five- to eight-year-olds. Begin with a good story, replay it in several different ways, and then write it down to create a script.

✔ **Director's Book** Create a director's book by cutting apart a script and photocopying the pages onto larger sheets of paper so there is space to write notes and plan blocking.

✔ **Reawaken Creativity** If a scene becomes stagnant, give students a new and unusual intention or focus, such as playing the scene in slow motion or in an angry manner.

✔ **Technical Preparations** Have students use real or temporary props in rehearsals as soon as possible. Always hold a technical rehearsal so lighting and sound technicians can practice. Practice the curtain call with actors.

✔ **Work as a Team** Encourage students to help each other out; if one student forgets a line, another should cover or ad-lib; if a sound effect is missed, students should improvise to keep the scene going.

Ideas for Cross-Curricular Theatre Activities

Social Studies

▶ Divide the class into two groups. Have one group reenact a historical event while the other group acts as a film crew presenting a message biased toward a particular viewpoint of this event. Let the tensions between the two groups mount as the drama unfolds.

▶ Have small groups of students re-create the daily family life of a tribe. At some point you should enter the scene and act as a government representative who tells them they have to leave their sacred lands. Each group should decide which object they will take with them on their journey and explain why. Allow them to confront the governmental official.

Math

▶ Any story problem in the curriculum has the potential for dramatization.

▶ Role-play a situation in which making change with play money is a natural part of the drama, perhaps taking place at imagined cash registers.

▶ Role-play restaurant visits and have students calculate the tips in their heads.

▶ Whenever a drama calls for an interior space, discuss square footage. For example, have students calculate how large a hospital must be if it has 100 rooms of 9' by 10'.

Science

▶ Have one group of students discover a negative, environmental impact of a development in a community, such as a factory or housing. Unfortunately the community is dependent on this development for its economic well-being. Allow the first group to confront other students portraying town leaders with the facts they have discovered.

▶ In small groups, have one student assume the role of an important scientist, such as Jonas Salk. Allow the others to portray people who question the validity or safety of this person's work. How does the scientist present his or her case to the larger community?

Reading/Writing

▶ Have readers write a diary entry for a character from a scene they have acted out.

▶ Have students write letters in role as one character addressing another, perhaps several years after the events in the story.

▶ Have students tell or write the story of what happened long ago in a certain building in the role of stones from that building.

An Overview of the History of Theatre

Western theatre is considered to have begun with the Dionysia, a huge dramatic festival that first appeared in fifth-century B.C. Greece. The festival was held in honor of Dionysus, the Greek god of wine and nature; it contained competitions for the best dramas. The first competitions were for tragedies, which were based on Greek mythology and told of the struggles and downfalls of central heroic characters. Tragedies were written in groups of three. Each could stand on its own, but together they formed a larger unity. The great Greek tragedy writers include Aeschylus, Sophocles, and Euripides. Soon a separate competition was added for comedies, which were also rooted in ritual and mythology, but concluded with happy outcomes and featured political or literary satire. Comic playwrights include Aristophanes and Menander. Both styles included musical accompaniment, and most plays had a chorus. Greek theatres were semicircular in shape and built into hillsides so that the seats rose up from the ground-level stage area, similar to a modern arena.

Roman theatre developed from the Greeks, who they conquered in the third century B.C. Many early Roman plays were translations and adaptations of Greek plays. However, while the Greeks preferred tragedy, comedy was more popular in Rome and was of a more vulgar nature than the satiric Greek comedy. Theatres were built on level ground instead of a hill and contained a raised stage with elaborate backdrops. Eventually the chorus was eliminated and a curtain was used for the first time. Entertainment in the first century A.D. turned to gladiatorial and nautical spectacles, and by the fifth century, Christian opposition to theatre virtually eliminated all forms of drama in the declining Roman Empire.

Western theatre appeared again in the Middle Ages when the Christian church that had originally opposed drama began using liturgical plays during Mass. In the eleventh century, medieval guilds began producing plays, which remained biblical. These plays were performed outdoors. Miracle plays (dramatizations of Christian miracles), mystery plays (which included bible stories), and morality plays (in which characters were personified virtues such as Truth) were all common.

A high point of European theatre came around the sixteenth century, when Renaissance drama developed and England experienced the Elizabethan period and the rise of William Shakespeare. The increasingly professional theatres could accommodate multiple plots and stage actions. The Globe Theatre (where Shakespeare's plays were performed) was an open-air octagonal theatre, with a large elevated stage, permanent backdrop, and roofed galleries for the audience. Shakespeare wrote tragedies, comedies, romances, and historical plays, including *Hamlet, Romeo and Juliet,* and *Henry V.*

After the Elizabethan period, enclosed theatres were built and European theatre became a more elite entertainment. Female actors appeared in legitimate English theatre for the first time. Professional acting companies developed throughout Europe, and by the eighteenth century, these companies were also in America.

The nineteenth-century Romantic era produced the melodrama, an emotional, excitement-driven play featuring the courageous hero, the innocent heroine, and the evil villain. In response to Romanticism, the French "well-made play" developed, which contained a tightly structured plot with a predictable beginning, middle, and end.

In the early twentieth century, modernist playwrights abandoned past dramatic traditions. Modernist plays followed the new style of realism, in which an invisible "fourth wall" was erected between stage and audience, and theatre strove to present a "slice of life." American drama today encompasses all eras, as theatre-goers can sample everything from modern adaptations of Greek tragedies to realistic Shakespearean reenactments.

Eastern theatre began much the same as theatre had in the West, with religious rituals. According to an ancient theatre handbook, Indian drama began when the creator god Brahma brought together song, dance, and recitation to please all social classes. Indian drama was reflexive, and not bound to the western idea that a play must have a set plot with rising action, climax, and resolution. The oldest surviving plays of this kind are the highly stylized Sanskrit plays from the first century A.D., which involved stock characters whose movements and physical responses were emphasized over speech. Sanskrit declined after the tenth-century Muslim invasions, and folk dramas became the popular theatre form. During the fifteenth-century Hindu cultural revival, regional dance dramas developed, as well as historical hero plays and social satires. These all play a role in modern Indian theatre.

Chinese drama also grew from religious roots, centering around gods and ancient ancestors. Other similarities to Indian drama include stock characters and the emphasis on physical performance over literary aspects. The height of Chinese drama came in the thirteenth and fourteenth centuries with the Zaju drama, a multi-act musical play in which all conflicts are resolved and peace is restored in the final act. During the sixteenth-century Ming Dynasty, most popular theatre was looked down upon by intellectuals. The exception was Kunqu, which took place in real time to bamboo flute music and took days to perform. Modern Chinese theatre began with the eighteenth century Peking (now Beijing) Opera. As in early Chinese traditions, the Peking opera used mythological and historical subject matter and focused on music and dance performances, but it added high-speed acrobatics and duels.

Ancient and modern Japanese theatre draws inspiration from Chinese legends, but its greatest influence is native culture. Unique to Japan is Noh drama, which dates from the fourteenth century. Noh features two actors, a singing chorus, and musicians. It has little or no plot or conflict and has no ties to realism. The Kabuki theatre of the seventeenth century catered more to the growing Japanese middle class. Kabuki, which means "singing-dancing-acting," features more individual acting roles and innovative stage machinery, such as the revolving stage, which was developed in Japan years before it was seen in the west.

Early African theatre, similar to its western and Asian counterparts, took form in religious rituals that included dancing, drumming, and mask work. Communal dancing and ceremonial performances were special events that involved all tribe members. Storytelling was another dramatic form in which spoken narration and dialogue was joined by music and dancing.

In the sixteenth century, African slaves brought their traditions to America, and a unique African American dramatic style developed from the original rituals. For example, clapping and foot tapping replaced African drums and eventually evolved into early American tap dancing. Many prominent African American playwrights appeared in the twentieth century, especially during the Harlem Renaissance. Today's theatre reflects a renewed interest in early African heritage.

Further Resources

Books and Articles

Arts Education Partnership (2002). Critical links: Learning in the arts and student academic and social development. Washington, D.C.: Arts Education Partnership.

Booth, D. H. (1987). Drama worlds: The role of drama in language growth. Toronto: Language Study Centre, Toronto Board of Education.

Booth, D. H. (1994). Story drama. Markham: Pembroke Publishers.

Byron, K. (1986). Drama in the English classroom. New York: Methuen.

Bailey, S. D. (1993). Wings to fly: Bringing theatre arts to students with special needs. Woodbine House.

Erion, P. & Lewis, J. C. (1996). Drama in the classroom: Creative activities for teachers, parents, and friends. Lost Coast Press.

Gardner, H. (1985). Towards a theory of dramatic intelligence. In J. Kase-Polisini (Ed.), Creative drama in a developmental context. New York: University Press of America.

Heathcote, D., & Bolton, G. (1995). Drama for learning: Dorothy Heathcote's mantle of the expert approach to education. Portsmouth, NH: Heinemann.

McCaslin, Nellie. (1999). Creative drama in the classroom. Pearson, Allyn, & Bacon.

Miller, C. S. & Saxton, J. (2004) Into the story: Language and action through drama. Portsmouth, NH: Heinemann.

Moffett, James & Wagner, Betty Jane. (1992). Student-centered language arts, K-12. Portsmouth, NJ: Boynton/Cook, Heinemann.

O'Neill, C. & Lambert, Alan. (1990). Drama structures: Practical handbook for teachers. Stanley Thornes Pub. Ltd.

Shah, A., & Joshi, U. (1992). Puppetry and folk dramas for non-formal education. Sterling Pub. Private Ltd.

Stewig, J. W. (1983). Informal drama in the elementary language arts program. New York: Teachers College Press.

Wagner, B. J. (1998). Educational drama and language arts: What research shows, third book in the Dimensions of Drama series. Portsmouth, NH: Heinemann.

Wagner, B. J. (1983). The expanding circle of informal classroom drama. In B. A. Busching & J. I. Schwartz (Eds.), Integrating the language arts in the elementary school (pp. 155–163). Urbana, IL: National Council of Teachers of English.

Wagner, B. J. (1990). Dramatic improvisation in the classroom. In S. Hynds & D. L. Rubin (Eds.), Perspectives on talk and learning (pp. 195–211). Urbana, IL: National Council of Teachers of English.

Wagner, B. J. (1999). Dorothy Heathcote: Drama as a learning medium, 2nd ed. Portland, ME: Calendar Islands Publishers.

Wilhelm, J. D., & Edmiston, B. (1998). Imagining to learn: Inquiry, ethics, and integration through drama. Portsmouth, NH: Heinemann.

Wolf, S., Edmiston, B. W., & Enciso, P. (1996). Drama worlds: Places of the heart, voice and hand in dramatic interpretation. In J. Flood, D. Lapp, & S. B. Heath (Eds.), Handbook of research on teaching literacy through the communicative and visual arts (pp. 492–505). New York: Simon and Schuster, Macmillan.

Web sites

American Alliance for Theatre and Education: **www.aate.com.** Offers opportunities for educators to get advocacy information and collaborate with other educators

Drama Education: A Global Perspective—Learning in, with and through Drama: **members.iinet.net.au/~kimbo2.** Contains lists of drama education resources, including downloadable lesson plans and class activities, compiled by a theatre educator

VSA arts: **www.vsarts.org.** Offers a number of free resources for arts educators

National Dissemination Center for Children with Disabilities (NICHCY): **www.nichcy.org/index.html.** Offers information on special education law (IDEA), agencies and resources for educators and parents (both national and state) and specific disabilities.

Scope and Sequence of Theatre Concepts

Plot	K	1	2	3	4	5	6
A Plot Is Events in a Story	U1OP, 1.1, 1.6	U1OP, 1.1, 1.6	U1OP, 1.1, 1.6	U1OP, 1.6	U1OP, 1.6	U1OP, 1.6	U1OP, 1.6
Plot and Sequence	U1OP, 1.1, 1.2, 1.3, 1.4, 1.6	U1OP, 1.1, 1.2, 1.3, 1.4, 1.6	U1OP, 1.1, 1.2, 1.4, 1.6,	U1OP, 1.1, 1.3, 1.5, 1.6	U1OP, 1.1 1.6	U1OP, 1.1	U1OP, 1.1
Beginning/Exposition	U1OP, 1.2,	U1OP, 1.2, 1.6		U1OP, 1.3, 1.6	U1OP, 1.1	1.1	1.2
Presents a Problem	U1OP, 1.3,	U1OP, 1.3,	U1OP, 1.3,	U1OP, 1.4, 1.6	U1OP, 1.3, 1.6	U1OP, 1.3, 1.6	U1OP, 1.3, 1.6
Presents a Major Dramatic Question						U1OP, 1.3, 1.6	U1OP, 1.3, 1.6
Complications			U1OP, 1.3	U1OP, 1.4, 1.6	U1OP, 1.4, 1.6	U1OP, 1.4, 1.6	U1OP, 1.4, 1.6
High Point/Climax				U1OP, 1.5, 1.6	U1OP, 1.5, 1.6	1.5, 1.6	1.5, 1.6
Problem's End/Resolution	U1OP, 1.4	U1OP, 1.3, 1.4, 1.6	U1OP, 1.4	1.5, 1.6	U1OP, 1.5, 1.6	1.5, 1.6	1.5, 1.6
Asking "What If?"	U1OP, 1.5	U1OP, 1.5	U1OP, 1.5	1.6	1.6	1.2	1.6
Plot and the Five Ws				1.2, 1.6	1.2, 1.6	1.2, 1.6	

Character	K	1	2	3	4	5	6
What Constitutes a Character	U2OP, 2.1, 2.2, 2.3, 2.6	U2OP, 2.1, 2.2, 2.3, 2.6	U2OP, 2.1, 2.6	U2OP	U2OP	U2OP	U2OP
Character and the Five Ws	U2OP			U2OP			
Actions and Feelings	U2OP, 2.4, 2.5, 2.6	U2OP, 2.4	U2OP, 2.2, 2.3	U2OP, 2.1, 2.4, 2.6	U2OP, 2.1, 2.3, 2.4, 2.6	2.3, 2.4, 2.6	U2OP, 2.1, 2.2
Motivations			U2OP, 2.4, 2.6	U2OP, 2.1, 2.6	U2OP, 2.3, 2.6	2.1, 2.6	2.1, 2.2, 2.6
Actions Produce Reactions		U2OP, 2.5, 2.6	U2OP, 2.5, 2.6	2.3, 2.6	2.3, 2.4, 2.6	2.1, 2.3, 2.6	2.1, 2.6
Characters Interrelate				2.2, 2.6	2.2, 2.6	2.4, 2.6	2.1, 2.2, 2.6
Protagonist and Antagonist						U2OP, 2.2, 2.6	U2OP, 2.2, 2.6
Characters Solve a Problem				U2OP, 2.5, 2.6	2.5, 2.6	2.5, 2.6	2.5, 2.6
Internal Characterization							2.3, 2.6
External Characterization							2.4, 2.6

Sound and Voice	K	1	2	3	4	5	6
Sound Can Tell a Story	U3OP, 3.1, 3.6	U3OP, 3.1, 3.6					
Sound Shows Setting	U3OP, 3.2, 3.4, 3.6	U3OP, 3.2, 3.4, 3.6	U3OP, 3.1, 3.6	U4OP, 4.1, 4.4, 4.6	U4OP, 4.2, 4.6	U4OP, 4.1, 4.4	U4OP, 4.3, 4.6
Sound Evokes Feelings			U3OP, 3.4	4.1, 4.6	U4OP, 4.4	U4OP, 4.1	U4OP, 4.1, 4.6
Music Evokes Feelings			U3OP, 3.2	U4OP, 4.2, 4.6	U4OP, 4.4	U4OP, 4.2	U4OP, 4.2
Voice Shows Emotion	U3OP, 3.3, 3.5, 3.6	U3OP, 3.3, 3.6	U3OP, 3.5, 3.6	U4OP, 4.5, 4.6	U4OP, 4.5, 4.6	4.5, 4.6	U4OP, 4.5, 4.6
Voice Shows Character	U3OP, 3.5, 3.6	U3OP, 3.5, 3.6	U3OP, 3.3, 3.6	4.3, 4.6	4.3, 4.6	4.3, 4.6	4.4, 4.6
Sound and Silence Communicate							4.1
Sound/Voice and the Five Ws				4.1	4.1	4.1, 4.3	

Visual Elements	K	1	2	3	4	5	6
Physically Showing Setting	U4OP, 4.1, 4.2, 4.6	U4OP, 4.1, 4.5, 4.6	5.1	3.1	5.3	5.1	5.1
Physically Showing Invisible Objects	U4OP, 4.3	U4OP, 4.2	5.5	3.1			
Creating Costumes	U4OP, 4.4, 4.6	U4OP, 4.3	U5OP, 5.2, 5.6	U3OP, 3.3, 3.6	5.4, 5.6	5.3, 5.6	5.2, 5.6
Creating Masks/Makeup		U4OP, 4.4, 4.6	5.6	3.4, 3.6	5.5, 5.6	5.4, 5.6	5.3, 5.6
Creating Setting	U4OP, 4.5, 4.6	U4OP, 4.5, 4.6	U5OP, 5.4, 5.6	U3OP, 3.5, 3.6	5.1, 5.3, 5.6	5.2, 5.6	5.4, 5.6
Creating Puppets			U5OP, 5.3	1.6, 5.3			
Choosing Props	U4OP, 4.6	4.6		3.2	5.2, 5.6	5.5, 5.6	5.5, 5.6
Visual Elements and the Five Ws				3.1, 3.6	5.3, 5.6	5.1, 5.6	

Movement	K	1	2	3	4	5	6
Realistic Movement	U5OP, 5.1, 5.6	U5OP, 5.2, 5.6	4.4, 4.6	U5OP, 5.1, 5.5, 5.6	U3OP, 3.2, 3.5, 3.6	U3OP, 3.2, 3.5, 3.6	U3OP, 3.1, 3.3, 3.5, 3.6
Abstract Movement						U3OP, 3.3	U3OP, 3.3
Rhythm	U5OP, 5.3, 5.6	U5OP, 5.1, 5.3, 5.6	U4OP, 4.1, 4.6	U5OP, 5.4, 5.6	3.4, 3.6	U3OP, 3.4	U3OP, 3.5, 3.6
Repetition	5.3		U4OP, 4.3	U5OP, 5.4, 5.6	3.4, 3.6	U3OP, 3.4	3.5
Shape and Form				5.3	3.3	3.1	3.1
Action and Inaction	U5OP, 5.5	5.4		5.2	3.1, 3.6	3.5	3.4
Action and Reaction		U5OP, 5.3	U4OP, 4.2	5.5, 5.6	3.5, 3.6	3.5	3.4, 3.6
Movement Communicates	U5OP, 5.1, 5.2, 5.4, 5.6	5.2, 5.5	U4OP, 4.4, 4.5, 4.6	U5OP, 5.1, 5.6	U3OP, 3.2, 3.6	3.2, 3.6	U3OP, 3.2, 3.6
Movement and the Five Ws				5.1	3.2	3.2	

Subject, Theme, and Mood	K	1	2	3	4	5	6
Creating Stories	6.1						
Analyzing Stories	U6OP, 6.2, 6.6	U6OP, 6.1, 6.6	U6OP, 6.1	U6OP, 6.1, 6.5, 6.6	U6OP, 6.2, 6.6	6.2, 6.3, 6.6	6.2, 6.5, 6.6
Discovering Subject	U6OP, 6.3, 6.6	U6OP, 6.2, 6.6	U6OP, 6.2, 6.6	6.1, 6.6	6.1, 6.6	U6OP, 6.1, 6.6	6.1, 6.6
Discovering Theme				6.3, 6.4, 6.5, 6.6	6.1, 6.2, 6.6	U6OP, 6.1, 6.2, 6.6	6.1, 6.5, 6.6
Discovering Mood	U6OP, 6.4, 6.5, 6.6	U6OP, 6.3	U6OP, 6.3, 6.6	6.2, 6.6	6.5, 6.6	U6OP, 6.3, 6.4, 6.6	6.2, 6.6
Showing Theme				6.3, 6.4, 6.6	6.4, 6.5, 6.6	6.5, 6.6	6.5, 6.6
Showing Mood	6.4, 6.5, 6.6	6.3, 6.4, 6.5, 6.6	6.4, 6.5, 6.6	6.2, 6.6	6.3, 6.4, 6.5	6.4, 6.5, 6.6	6.3, 6.4, 6.6
Subject and Five Ws	U6OP			6.1	6.1	6.1	
Theme and the Five Ws				6.2	6.1	6.1	

Scope and Sequence of Theatre Activities

Creative Expression Activity Type	K	1	2	3	4	5	6
Theatre Game	1.1, 1.4, 2.1, 2.5, 3.1, 3.5, 6.2	1.1, 2.5, 3.3, 4.1, 5.3	1.1, 2.2, 3.5, 4.2, 5.1	1.4, 2.3, 5.2	1.1, 4.2, 6.1	6.1	1.1
Improvisation	1.3, 2.2, 2.3, 3.3, 4.1, 5.1, 6.5	1.3, 2.1, 2.6, 3.1, 3.5, 4.2, 4.6, 6.1, 6.6	1.3, 1.4, 2.1, 3.3, 4.3, 5.5, 6.2	1.2, 2.5, 4.3, 4.5, 5.5	1.2, 2.3, 2.4, 4.5, 6.5	1.2, 1.4, 2.2, 2.4, 3.4, 4.3, 4.5, 6.5	1.2, 2.2, 2.5, 3.4, 4.5, 4.6, 6.1, 6.5
Pantomime	2.4, 4.3, 5.2	1.2, 5.2	1.2, 2.5	1.3, 5.1, 5.6, 6.4	3.5, 3.6	1.3, 3.5, 3.6, 5.1	1.3, 2.4, 3.2, 3.6, 5.1, 6.3
Tableau	4.2, 5.5, 6.4	2.4, 5.4	2.4	2.2, 5.6	1.5, 2.2, 3.1		6.4
Puppets			2.6, 5.3	1.6			
Shadow Puppets				5.3			
Play Writing/Recording Dialogue	6.6	6.6	6.6	2.6, 6.6	2.6, 6.6	2.6, 6.6	2.6, 6.6
Storytelling	1.2, 1.6, 3.6, 6.1	1.4, 1.5,	1.5, 1.6, 6.3	1.1, 2.4,	1.3, 4.3,	1.1	1.4, 4.4
Reader's Theatre				1.5		4.4, 4.6	1.5
Creative Movement	1.5, 5.3, 5.6, 6.3	5.1, 5.6, 6.4	3.2, 4.1, 4.6, 6.5	3.1, 4.2, 5.4,	3.3, 3.4	3.1, 3.3, 6.4	3.3, 4.2, 6.2
Dramatic Movement	2.6, 5.4	2.2, 5.5, 6.3	2.3, 4.4, 4.5	2.1, 6.2	2.1, 3.2	2.5, 3.2, 4.2, 6.3	3.1, 3.5
Sensory/Emotional Recall						2.1, 2.3, 2.6	2.1, 2.3, 2.6
Creation of Sound Effects	3.2, 3.4, 3.6	3.2, 3.4, 3.6, 6.5	3.1, 3.4, 3.6	4.1, 4.4, 4.6	4.1, 4.4, 4.6	4.1, 4.4, 4.6	4.1, 4.3, 4.6
Creation of Setting	4.5, 4.6	4.6	5.4	3.5, 3.6, 6.5	5.1, 5.3, 5.6, 6.3	5.2, 5.6	5.4, 5.6
Creation/Selection of Costumes	4.4	4.3	5.2	3.3, 3.6	5.4, 5.6	5.3, 5.6	5.2, 5.6
Creation/Selection of Props				3.2, 3.6	5.2, 5.6	5.5, 5.6	5.5, 5.6
Creation of Makeup Designs				3.4	5.5, 5.6	5.4, 5.6	5.3, 5.6
Creation of Masks			4.4	5.6			
Script/Story Dramatization		1.6, 2.3, 3.6, 6.2	2.6, 3.6, 4.6, 5.6, 6.1, 6.4	1.6, 2.6, 3.6, 4.6, 5.6, 6.1, 6.3, 6.6	1.4, 1.6, 2.5, 2.6, 3.6, 4.6, 5.6, 6.4	1.5, 1.6, 2.6, 4.6, 5.6, 6.2	1.4, 1.6, 2.6, 3.6, 5.6, 6.6
Direction of Others			6.4	6.3	6.4	6.5	6.5

Glossary

A

acting portraying a character to tell a story

action everything characters do in a play

action/reaction the interplay between characters in which the action of the plot is moved forward

actor a person who portrays a character in a play

antagonist a character opposing the protagonist, or leading character

arena stage a stage surrounded by audience seating

artistic license the idea that an author or performing artist has a right to change a story's details to fit his or her conception of the story's theme and to make it work better as a plot

audience a group of people assembled to see a performance

B

blocking traveling movement onstage planned and created by directors, actors, and stage managers

C

character a person in a story, play, or poem; can be a personified animal or object

choreographer a person who plans dance movements in dance, opera, and certain theatre productions

chorus a group of actors who narrate the action of a play

climax the point in a plot where the interest, tension, and excitement are highest

comedy a humorous genre of theatre developed by ancient Greeks

complication a new event or character in the story that makes a problem more difficult to solve

conflict the problem or struggle in a story

costume the clothing, accessories, and makeup or mask worn by an actor in a play

costume designer a person who creates costumes for the actors to wear in a play

D

decorative prop an object, such as a framed portrait, used to reveal a play's setting but not used by an actor

dialogue speech between characters in a play

director the person who unifies all the elements of a play to create an artistic production

dramaturge a consultant, often employed by a theatre, who is familiar with a play, its history, other productions of a play, the playwright's other works and so on; assists in research and evaluation

E

emotional recall the technique of using emotional memories in the process of characterization

enunciation clear and distinct pronunciation

environmental sound effects sounds that convey setting and environment

exposition information in a play or story, usually revealed near the beginning, that sets up the plot's action

external complication a physical event that occurs in a play that makes a problem more difficult to solve

F

five Ws five questions that a plot can answer: *who, what, when, where, why*

five Ws and an H six questions that a plot can answer: *who, what, when, where, why, how*

floor properties objects, such as a sofa, table, or lamp, found onstage

full back stance an actor's position onstage when his or her back is to the audience

full front stance an actor's position onstage when he or she faces the audience

I

inaction a purposeful pause in onstage action

incidental music background music used to create various moods

inflection a change in pitch and volume of a voice

integral music music that is written into a script to help motivate action, sometimes played by an actor onstage

internal complication a feeling or attitude within a character that makes a problem more difficult to solve

L

lighting the use of colored gel sheets to create realistic lighting or mood lighting onstage to reveal the *when* and *where* of a play

lighting designer a person who designs the lighting for a play, both for basic illumination and for effect

lighting director the person who is in charge of running lighting

live sounds sounds created during a performance that are not prerecorded

M

Major Dramatic Question the main question presented in drama; the action of the play serves to address and answer this question

makeup cosmetic elements used to highlight or alter an actor's face

makeup artist a person who uses makeup to change an actor's appearance

mask a costume piece that covers the face

mechanical sound effects sounds used to motivate action, such as a ringing doorbell

mime an actor who uses body movements and facial expressions to portray a character or situation

minimalism a theatrical movement in which setting, gesture, and dialogue are stripped down to essentials

monologue a speech, often lengthy, spoken by one character

mood the emotional feelings experienced by the audience and created by a performance

motivation a character's reason for speech or action

O

objective the goal a character works toward in a scene; part of a character's major goal in a play

onstage on the visible stage

P

personal prop an object held and used by a character

physicality a focus on physical movement that suggests age, emotion, or physical condition

playwright a person who writes the action, dialogue, and directions for movement in a play

plot a sequence of events that forms a story or drama

presentational theatre an approach to theatre in which it is obvious that the play is not like real life

producer a person responsible for a play, movie, or show; he or she obtains the script, raises money, and finds the theatre for the production

profile stance an actor's position onstage when he or she is turned sideways from the audience

projection speaking with enough vocal force to allow an audience to clearly hear what is said

properties also called *props;* objects found onstage

proscenium stage a stage framed by an arch, forming a box with three sides

protagonist the leading character in a play

puppet an object brought to life for an audience

Q

quarter stance an actor's position onstage when he or she is turned a quarter left or right away from facing the audience

R

recorded sound a sound effect that is recorded and played during a performance

repetition in theatrical movement, a pattern of repeated movement

representational characterization an acting technique in which actors represent characters' thoughts and feelings through movement and costumes

representational theatre an approach to theatre in which the audience "suspends disbelief" and views the performance as real life

resolution the part of the plot, usually near the end, in which the plot's problems are solved

rhythm in theatre, an orderly or irregular pattern of movements; also the pace of a character or play

rising action the part of a play, usually at the beginning, in which a main problem is introduced

role the part or character that an actor performs

S

satire an ironic, farcical genre of theatre developed by ancient Greeks

scenario the outline of action in a play

scenery painted boards, screens, or three-dimensional units that form the background of a play and enclose the acting area

scenic designer a person who develops the environment for the action of the play

script a copy of a play that provides stage directions and dialogue

sensory recall the use of remembered sights, sounds, tastes, and textures when portraying a character

set the scenery, props, and furniture onstage; also a term for placing props or scenery

set designer a person who creates scenery for many types of productions

sound designer a person who decides how and when sound effects will be used in a theatrical performance

sound effects sounds and music used onstage

sound technician a person skilled at using sound equipment to create the special sound effects needed in a play or performance

spike to mark the location of large props with small pieces of tape onstage

stage crew backstage workers, including stagehands or grips, who handle scenery, and the prop crew, who handle properties

stage manager a person who helps the director and actors by writing down blocking, scheduling, and overseeing the technical aspects of a production

stock character a character whose feelings and actions come from cultural stereotypes, for example, a crazy scientist or a damsel in distress

storyteller a person who remembers the order of events in a story and tells it to listeners in a narrative style

strike to remove props quickly from a set

subject what a play is about, usually an abstract concept such as truth

subtext the character's inner feelings and intentions not expressed directly

synopsis a brief, general review or summary

T

technical production includes stage management, lighting, sound, stage mechanics, promotions, set design, and directing

theatre-in-the-round a type of theatre in which an audience can sit around all four sides of the stage

theme the message a play or drama communicates about its subject, such as "greed will lead to trouble"

thrust stage a low, platform stage that projects into the audience

tone the use of inflection to communicate feelings

tragedy a type of drama, created by ancient Greeks, in which a protagonist comes into conflict with a greater force or person and ends with a sad, disastrous conclusion

U

universal character a character type who appears in stories and literature throughout the world

V

visual elements the aspects of a dramatic performance that the audience sees, including costumes, props, scenery, lighting, makeup, and puppets

Glossary

Program Index

Items referenced are coded by Grade Level and page number.

A

abstract movement **L5** 52, 58–59; **L6** 52, 58–59, 64

acting **L1** 35; **L3** 17, 35

actor **LK** 34–51; **L2** 49; **L4** 35, 49, 116–117; **L5** 35, 49; **L6** 16, 64, 89

antagonist **L5** 34, 38–39, 46–47, 97; **L6** 34–35, 38–39, 46, 48

anti-heroes **L3** 112

arena stage **L5** 92; **L6** 112

artistic license **L5** 82

B

backdrop **L4** 90; **L5** 101; **L6** 101

ballad opera **L5** 74

blocking **LK** 103; **L3** 89; **L4** 53; **L5** 52; **L6** 63, 67

C

cause-and-effect **L6** 26

character **LK** 34–51, 107; **L1** 34–52; **L2** 34–51, 58, 65; **L3** 17, 34–51, 76–77, 89, 114–115; **L4** 17, 34–51, 88–89, 100–101; **L5** 34–51; **L6** 34–51, 54, 64, 66, 114–115

charades **L1** 20, 89

choral reading **L2** 83; **L4** 110

choreographer **L1** 89, 103; **L4** 53, 67, 121; **L5** 60, 67, 114; **L6** 74, 120

chorus **L5** 26

climax **L1** 29; **L3** 17, 26–27; **L4** 16–17, 26–29; **L5** 17, 26–27, 29–30; **L6** 16–17, 26–29

comedy **L2** 76, 112; **L3** 76, 98; **L4** 112; **L5** 18; **L6** 110, 118

commedia dell'arte **L2** 98; **L3** 98

complication **L2** 22; **L3** 16, 24–25, 29–30; **L4** 17, 24–25, 28–29; **L5** 16–17, 24–25, 29–30; **L6** 17, 24–25, 28–29

conflict **LK** 16; **L4** 24, 28–30; **L5** 24, 30; **L6** 24

costume designer **LK** 85; **L1** 49; **L2** 103; **L3** 67, 83; **L4** 103, 112; **L5** 89; **L6** 49

costumes **LK** 70–71, 78, 82–83, 85, 92, 116, 118; **L1** 70–71, 76–77, 82–84, 107; **L2** 88–89, 92–93, 100, 103; **L3** 52–53, 58–59, 64, 101; **L4** 88–89, 96–97, 100–101, 112, 114, 118; **L5** 88–89, 94–95, 100–101; **L6** 88–89, 92–93, 100–101

creative movement **LK** 94, 100, 112; **L1** 100–103; **L2** 72, 82–85; **L3** 74; **L4** 58; **L6** 58, 74, 110

D

designers **L2** 89

dialect coach **L6** 85

dialogue **LK** 119–120; **L1** 29, 72, 78, 108, 118–121; **L2** 17, 29, 98; **L3** 17, 76, 80–81; **L4** 17, 41; **L5** 42

diaphragm **L5** 70

director **LK** 107, 116, 121; **L1** 31; **L2** 71, 85, 106–107, 114–115, 118; **L3** 31, 107, 112–113; **L4** 107, 121; **L5** 53, 116–119; **L6** 16, 85, 89, 107–108, 116–117

drama **L2** 92; **L4** 112; **L6** 110

dramatic movement **LK** 46; **L1** 38; **L2** 40, 80; **L3** 36, 110; **L4** 36, 60, 110; **L5** 44, 56, 74, 112; **L6** 54, 62

dramaturge **L6** 85, 107–108

E

emotion **L1** 36; **L3** 88; **L4** 71; **L5** 58; **L6** 54–55, 74

emotional recall **L5** 40, 101; **L6** 40, 46–47

enunciation **L5** 76; **L6** 80

exposition **L6** 16–17, 20–21, 28–29

external characterization **L6** 35, 42–43

external complications **L5** 24

F

facial expressions **LK** 44, 114, 120; **L1** 88–89, 100; **L2** 26, 80; **L3** 24–25, 53, 89, 100; **L4** 116; **L5** 58, 96, 112; **L6** 53, 56, 64–65

farce **L6** 110

T38 Teacher's Handbook

five *W*s **LK** 34, 106; **L3** 20–21, 34, 54–55, 72–73, 90–91, 108–111; **L4** 20–21, 29, 56–57, 72–73, 88, 94–95, 108–109; **L5** 20–21, 28–29, 56–57, 72–73, 76–77, 90–91, 108–109

H

history plays **L6** 118

horror **L4** 112

I

improvisation **LK** 22, 38, 58, 72, 116; **L1** 22, 36, 46–49, 62, 74, 78, 108; **L2** 22, 24, 36, 58, 76, 98, 100; **L3** 36, 44, 47, 65, 76, 80, 98; **L4** 20, 29, 40, 42, 80, 100–103, 114, 119; **L5** 24, 38, 42, 60, 76, 80, 90, 116; **L6** 20, 29, 36, 38, 44, 60, 72, 78, 82–85, 96, 108, 116

incidental music **L3** 71; **L6** 71

inflection **L3** 70, 80–81; **L4** 70, 80–82; **L5** 70, 80–82; **L6** 80–81

integral music **L3** 71

intellectual method **L5** 110

internal characterization **L6** 35, 40–41

internal complications **L5** 24

L

lighting **LK** 71, 116, 118; **L1** 107, 121; **L2** 89, 107; **L3** 53; **L5** 90, 100, 107; **L6** 100–101, 113

lighting designer **LK** 58; **L1** 121; **L3** 103

M

Major Dramatic Question **L5** 16–17, 22–23, 29; **L6** 16–17, 22–23

makeup **LK** 71; **L1** 70–71, 82, 85; **L2** 88–89, 100; **L3** 52–53, 60–61, 64; **L4** 88–89, 98–101; **L5** 88–89, 96–97, 100, 103; **L6** 88–89, 94–95, 100–101

makeup artist **L1** 85; **L3** 49; **L5** 203; **L6** 94

masks **L1** 70, 76, 78–79, 82, 85; **L2** 100–102; **L3** 52–53, 60, 67; **L4** 88, 98–99; **L5** 118; **L6** 94

melodrama **L5** 38; **L6** 110

Method acting **L5** 35; **L6** 40

mime **LK** 42, 76, 92; **L1** 74, 92; **L3** 24; **L5** 29

minimalism **L1** 72

monologue **L4** 46–49; **L5** 46–47, 108; **L6** 46–49

mood **LK** 53, 90, 106–123; **L1** 52–53, 71, 82, 90, 100, 106–123; **L2** 53, 103, 106–123; **L3** 53, 70–71, 74, 106–123; **L4** 52, 64, 70, 78, 82, 84, 88, 100, 106–123; **L5** 70, 74, 82, 88–89, 100, 106–123; **L6** 71–72, 100, 106–123

motivation **L2** 34, 42, 46; **L3** 34, 36; **L4** 36; **L5** 36; **L6** 36, 46–47

musical comedy **L5** 97

musical theatre **L4** 67; **L6** 74

mystery **L6** 110

N

narrative pantomime **L3** 58, 101; **L5** 119; **L6** 83

narrator **LK** 29, 62; **L2** 56; **L5** 29–30, 119

O

objective **L5** 38; **L6** 36

objects **L1** 74–75; **L2** 98–99

obstacles **L5** 30; **L6** 48

offstage action **LK** 53

onomatopoeia **L6** 72

P

pantomime **LK** 18, 42, 76, 90, 92, 101, 112; **L1** 20, 24, 92, 94; **L2** 20, 44; **L3** 22, 24, 58, 72, 89–90, 100–104, 114; **L4** 36, 62, 65; **L5** 22, 46–47, 62, 64–66, 82–83, 90, 108, 119; **L6** 22, 42, 53, 56, 64–65, 74, 83, 90, 112

parody **L6** 110

physicality **L6** 42

pitch **L5** 80

playbill **L5** 121

playwright **LK** 17, 31, 35, 107; **L1** 17, 107, 110; **L2** 31; **L3** 17, 106, 121; **L4** 17, 31, 66, 102–103, 106, 119; **L5** 17, 31; **L6** 16–17, 20, 80, 89, 103, 107, 114, 118

plot **LK** 16–33, 107; **L1** 16–33, 52; **L2** 16–33, 47; **L3** 16–33; **L4** 16–33; **L5** 16–33; **L6** 16–33, 119

point of view **L4** 118

presentational theatre **L6** 106, 114

problem **L3** 16, 24–25, 28–30; **L4** 16–17, 22–23, 26, 28–29, 44–45; **L5** 19, 25, 44–45; **L6** 44–45

problem-solving **L4** 44–45; **L5** 19, 44–45; **L6** 44–45

producer **L1** 67; **L2** 49; **L4** 121; **L6** 121

production design **L6** 89

projection **L1** 52, 54, 64; **L5** 70, 76; **L6** 70, 80–81

promotional materials **L6** 108

promotions **L2** 107

prop crew **L6** 98

props **LK** 40, 70–71, 82–83, 116; **L1** 28, 70–71, 83; **L2** 88–89, 100; **L3** 52–53, 56–57, 62, 64,

101; **L4** 88–89, 92–93, 100–101, 114, 118, 120; **L5** 88, 98, 100–101, 107; **L6** 16, 65, 88–89, 98–101, 113

proscenium stage **L5** 92; **L6** 112

protagonist **L5** 34, 38–39, 46–47; **L6** 34–35, 38–39

publicist **L5** 121; **L6** 108

puppet **LK** 62, 71; **L1** 28, 119; **L2** 47, 56, 89, 94–95; **L3** 28–29, 94–95

R

radio drama **L1** 56, 119; **L3** 78; **L4** 44, 74; **L5** 85; **L6** 72

Reader's Theatre **L3** 82–85, 132–136; **L5** 78, 82–85, 118–119

repetition **L2** 70, 76–77, 82, 108; **L3** 88, 96, 100, 102; **L4** 52, 60–61; **L5** 52, 60–61, 64; **L6** 62–63

representational characterization **L6** 42

representational theatre **L6** 106, 114

resolution **L4** 16–17, 26–29; **L5** 17, 22, 26–27, 29–30; **L6** 16–17, 26–29

S

satire **L5** 18, 74; **L6** 110

scenery **LK** 53, 70–72, 82–83, 92, 116, 118; **L1** 70–71, 82–83; **L2** 88–89, 100; **L3** 53–54, 62, 101, 116; **L4** 88, 90, 100–101, 114; **L5** 89, 92, 100–101, 107; **L6** 16, 88–89, 96, 100–101, 113

scenic designer **L1** 71; **L5** 89, 107; **L6** 31, 49

screenwriter **L4** 66

script **LK** 31, 103, 107, 118; **L1** 67; **L2** 29; **L3** 17, 71; **L4** 17, 20, 107, 118–119; **L5** 26; **L6** 65, 80, 85, 103

sensory recall **L5** 36; **L6** 36, 46–47

set designers **LK** 58; Set **L2** 89; **L3** 62, 64; **L4** 94, 103; **L5** 107; **L6** 31, 62, 98

setting **LK** 72, 80–81; **L1** 72, 107; **L2** 47, 88–91, 96–97, 100–101; **L3** 17, 62–63, 70, 78–79; **L4** 70–72, 74–75, 82, 85, 88–91, 94, 100; **L5** 70, 78–79, 82, 88–89, 92–93; **L6** 76–77, 88–91, 96–97, 112–113

shadow puppets **L2** 94; **L3** 94–95

silent films **L5** 76; **L6** 56

slapstick comedy **L3** 98

sound designer **LK** 67; **L2** 67; **L3** 85; **L4** 71, 85; **L6** 71, 77

sound effects **LK** 53, 56, 60; **L1** 52–53, 56, 60, 64–65, 67, 119; **L2** 52–53, 60, 64–66; **L3** 17, 70–73; **L4** 70–72, 85; **L5** 70, 72–73, 82, 85; **L6** 65, 70–71, 76, 82–83, 113

sound technicians **L5** 85; **L6** 71–72

stage crew **L6** 88, 96

stage directions **L3** 17; **L4** 60; **L5** 53; **L6** 62-63

stage manager **LK** 103; **L2** 121; **L6** 67

stock character **L4** 36; **L5** 38

storyboard **LK** 118; **L2** 119; **L6** 121

storytellers **L3** 20, 24, 88, 96

storytelling **LK** 28–31, 64–67; **L1** 18, 22; **L2** 28–31; **L4** 22, 76, 85; **L6** 24, 78

subject **LK** 106–123; **L1** 106–123; **L2** 103, 106–123; **L3** 106–123; **L4** 106–123; **L5** 106–123; **L6** 106–123

subtext **L6** 70, 78

T

tableau **LK** 74, 83, 98, 114; **L1** 42, 80, 83, 96; **L2** 42, 83; **L3** 38, 47; **L4** 38, 47, 54, 94, 108, 116; **L5** 112; **L6** 114

technical design **LK** 89; **L2** 89

technical production **L2** 107

theatre-in-the-round **LK** 80

theme **L3** 53, 106–123; **L4** 94, 106–123; **L5** 89, 106–123; **L6** 66, 92, 100–101, 106–123

thrust stage **L5** 92; **L6** 112

tone **L2** 52, 56; **L3** 70, 80–81; **L4** 70–71, 80–82, 84; **L5** 70, 80–82; **L6** 70, 80–81

tragedy **L2** 112; **L3** 76; **L5** 18; **L6** 110, 118

U

universal characters **L3** 36; **L6** 78

V

villain **L5** 97

visual elements **LK** 70–71, 82–83, 85, 107, 118; **L1** 70–87, 106–107, 118; **L2** 88–105; **L3** 52–69; **L4** 88–105; **L5** 88–105; **L6** 65, 88–105

voice coach **L6** 85

voice **LK** 52–69, 83, 107, 116, 118; **L1** 52–69; **L2** 35, 52–69; **L3** 70–87; **L4** 70–87; **L5** 70–87; **L6** 70–87

volume **L2** 52, 60; **L5** 80

Notes

Notes

Notes

Notes

Notes

Notes

Notes

Notes

Notes

Notes

Notes

Notes